COACHING THE
FLEX 1-3-3-1-3
ADAPTABLE TACTICS FOR THE MODERN GAME

by Wayne Harrison

Library of Congress
Cataloging - in - Publication Data

Coaching the Flex 1-3-3-1-3: Adaptable Tactics for the Modern Game
by Wayne Harrison

ISBN-13: 978-1-59164-248-0
Library of Congress Control Number: 2015953635
© 2015

Front cover photograph © PA/John Walton

Art Direction, Layout and Proofing
Bryan R. Beaver

Reedswain Publishing
88 Wells Road
Spring City, PA 19475
www. reedswain.com
orders@reedswain.com

Contents

The changing game now and in the future

The game is changing and we all must keep up with the changes happening if we are to provide a real service to the players. In my opinion this should start at youth level. But is it? Or will it?

To implement change means sometimes taking a step back to go a step or two forward, but that also means perhaps losing a few games in the process as we implement the education process of a new era in soccer. Unfortunately, this is something which many clubs and Directors of Coaching and even Club Presidents will not want to do, as each of you reading this are no doubt aware. In today's youth soccer culture, as well as all sports at youth level, the obsession with winning (and at all costs) too often outweighs the importance of teaching the game correctly.

This is a real shame, and I appeal to those out there who have bought this book to be brave, do not worry about results, explain what you are doing and why you are doing it to everyone involved. If the game is to progress in the way it needs to at youth level, it is VITAL that those in charge of our young players buy into the fact that player development is paramount and winning games CANNOT be the number one priority! Develop players correctly, teach them the right principles of play which I include in this book, and don't worry about the W / L columns. If you are able to do this then the wins will come (in time) but will also come in the RIGHT way by playing the RIGHT way and you will have given each player an incredible chance to progress in the RIGHT way in the game.

Therefore, the education provided as such has to be included for everyone involved; Coaching Directors, coaches, players, and most importantly parents, who often are held at arm's length for fear of coaches being challenged by educated people and not having answers to their questions. Easier to keep them in the dark and just take their money. I would add Club Presidents to this as we need as many people in charge to have a real understanding of the game. This is an underlying massive problem with the game at youth level.

Previously, teams played with rigidness, players staying in position with specialists in particular positions plying their trade. Now the game is becoming very fluid, flexible, interchangeable, rotational and with synchronization and therefore we must develop multi functional players who are able to play multiple roles within the team.

To this end, we teach players to be comfortable on the ball in a number of different positions to suit the philosophy of the team. Using tactics such as our Flex 1-3-3-1-3, players will often find themselves appearing in quite different positions than their starting positon and they need to be able to adjust and adapt to this and be successful doing it.

Beyond the system / formation of the team, it is about style, and this rotational and interchanging of positions on the field is the major change we are observing in the modern world game. This STYLE, which I call the **FLEX**, can actually be implemented in any system / formation you can use. Therefore, we are discussing here in this book a STYLE, or you can call it a PHILOSOPHY of how to play the game.

Bayern Munich manager Pep Guardiola (Ex Barcelona Manager and a genius in the development of the game) is perhaps the greatest proponent of this as he keeps reinventing the wheel with his innovative and forward thinking systems of play. While at Barcelona, 4-3-3 was his chosen system, though he sometimes adapted to 3-4-3. With Bayern Munich, he has moved to a 3-3-1-3 (3-1-3-3) and also 2-3-2-3. Here in this book we will focus on the 3-3-1-3. But it is not really about the numbers, it is about playing style. Every Barcelona and Bayern Munich player can and will change position and role according to the situation on the pitch. So, the numbers are merely a starting point as during the course of the match they are changing constantly.

Louis Van Gaal, manager of Manchester United stated: "You have to play as a team, you must create multi-functional players, able to play with both feet, have both defensive and offensive capabilities, be physically strong, quick, and have the necessary tactical acumen to function smoothly in rotational football, and ABOVE ALL, put their skills in service of the team effort".

Ok, not all players have everything, but we as coaches need to recognize the strengths and weaknesses of each player and fit them into the team style in the best way possible.

Some coaches may feel threatened by this new reality. Are they losing control? Is the game now about players' decision making over the coaches? The way I see it, we as coaches set up the framework from within which the players make the decisions. In this case we set up the 3-3-1-3 framework, we teach players various ideas to use within it and THEY decide when, where, how and why to use them.

This book is aimed at youth teams but also at professional level and senior teams; all can benefit from the information provided and coaches can use it to the extent that each of their teams at whatever level of play can understand.

The Playing Style (or Philosophy of Team Play)

Keep Possession:
If players chase for the ball a long time they get frustrated and commit fouls. So keep possession and force this upon the opponent. This is OUR form of defense. We keep the ball and get rested by doing so, the opponents chase the ball and get tired by doing so.

Develop Play from the back:
When it is on to do so to help maintain possession of the ball and not rely on a 2nd ball pick up

Pass and Move:
Movement off the ball is a major part of our team development

Form triangles and diamonds of support all over the field:
Creating open body stances and increasing peripheral awareness

Rotate & Inter-Change Positions:
Offensively and defensively cover for each other

Create space for your teammates, not just for yourself:
Unselfish team play; Play for the TEAM

Attacking Fullbacks - use Width in Attack:
Offense is the best form of defense

Keep a very high line defensively:
Squeeze opponents into their own half of the field and try to have no more than 25 yards from front to back

Pressure opponents high up the field:
Winning the ball back 20-30 yards from the opponent's goal is better than 80 yards away

Counter Attack and Quick Breakaway:
Developing different ways to counter attack

You need skilful players to make this all work:
We have the raw material so let's develop them

How Chile Played under coach Marcelo Bielsa

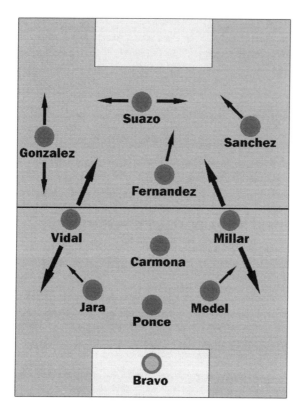

One of the National teams to play this way was Chile with Marcelo Bielsa in 2010. This was the basic set up, which can be seen as a 3-3-1-3, a 3-1-3-3 or 3–diamond-3.

Pep Guardiola, formerly of Barcelona and currently at Bayern Munich, experiments at times using this as well as other systems of play. So with this in mind I believe it is time to discuss 3-3-1-3 in full through this book, as top coaches start to look at how it works.

Guardiola is one of the top managers in the world of soccer and at the same time is a great admirer of Bielsa, so I believe it is time to look at this system of play in more depth.

Perhaps this is the future of Soccer?

In possession: Marcelo Bielsa tactics

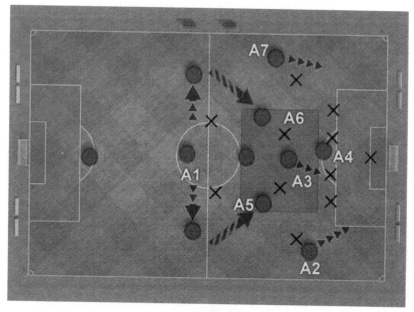

It is the fullbacks / wing backs who normally attack wide that cut inside to attack and form a diamond attack with (9) and (10) and the wingers stay wide. Alternatively, it can be the wingers who cut inside and the wing backs stay wide.

Out of possession: Marcelo Bielsa tactics

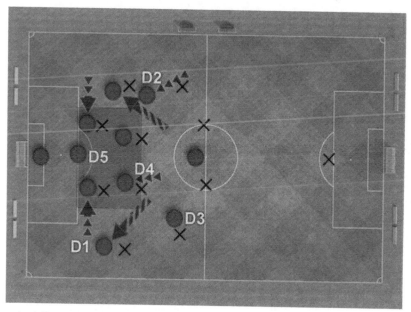

Here the fullbacks / wing backs drop back into a back 5 outside the central three defenders. They can also move inside to form a 2nd line of four in midfield with (8) and (10).

How Bayern Munich sometimes played
under coach Pep Guardiola

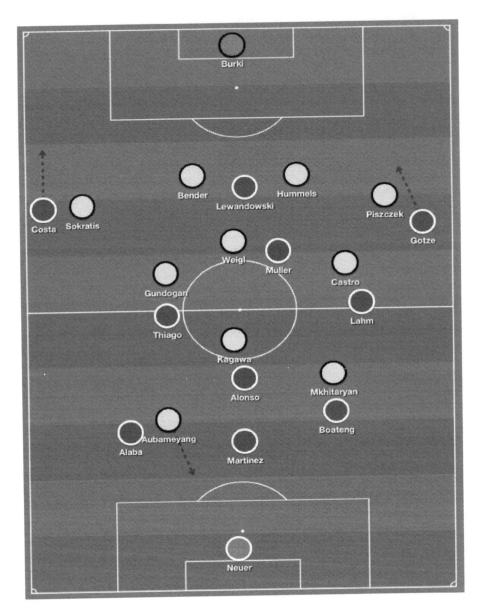

Note the fullbacks / WING BACKS OF Bayern tuck in to overload the center and middle of the field (Thiago and Lahm).

One can also have these two players touchline wide when in possession to spread out the midfield and open up spaces between opponents to play through.

The same can apply to right and left center backs breaking touchline wide also so we have 3 players in wide areas on both sides of the field in possession of the ball.

Introduction

The Flex 3-3-1-3 is a dynamic attacking system of play and I am excited to bring it to coaches from around the world to get their views on it. The one big difference in this way of playing is in terms of the wing fullbacks, whose positioning defensively can be VERY different to the normal wing fullback set up. In the normal set up the wing fullbacks play wide and tuck in defensively in the back line (usually a back 4), but in the 3-1-3-3 they tuck in defensively in the 2nd line of defense, working with #8 and #10 to form a defensive midfield four, asking the #10 to drop back to help. Or he stays up and the fullbacks #2 and #3 tuck in with #8 to form the 3-3-1-3.

The 3-3-1-3 is not a new system. In fact, it is more like an older, perhaps slightly forgotten about system that deserves to be back to the attention of world football. Bielsa has played it at International Level with Chile and made it into a very attractive and thought provoking way to play.

The Flex 3-3-1-3 changes constantly in transition. It can be a 3-3-1-3, 3-4-3 or 2-3-2-3 depending on the moment, or even a 5-4-1 in an ultimate defensive set up. The way I like to play this system is of course shown in this book, and is perhaps different to other interpretations, but this how I like to teach it.

The start position of the Flex 3-3-1-3 is very much like the 4-2-3-1 attacking phase 2 of play as shown in one of my previous books "Coaching the 4-2-3-1". We cover the attacking and defensive principles of the 3-3-1-3 here with the focus being on team preparation.

Like any system of play, the 3-3-1-3 has its strengths and weaknesses. The main weakness in my opinion is defensively down the flanks as we use three defenders with our wing backs #2 and #3 both pushed on to attack and then pushed into central midfield as our first defensive option on losing the ball, unless of course the ball is close to those players in particular.

I have included a section in this book on how we can teach the back players to adjust in ADVANCE of the ball being lost in certain areas of the field when we are attacking to ensure the immediate area the opponents are "likely" to play into is covered. I am presenting it as a possession based system of play, so your teams must have good technical ability to try it and of course high tactical IQ, or "Soccer Awareness" as I call it, to understand how it works.

It is not an easy choice to implement this system, but it is an exciting way to play and a challenge to coaches and players alike. The rotational elements in the book can be applied in any system of play really, they are just ideas to work on to develop freedom of play. Spatial awareness is a major teaching factor that players need to learn. This is essentially a posh way to say "movement off the ball", but nonetheless we must teach players to position on the field when in possession in terms of where the space is, what the opponents' positions are, and the positions of their team mates, and all this in advance of the ball (this is covered in my book "Soccer Awareness: Developing the Thinking Player").

We also discuss in simple detail how to play against different systems of play and how to cope when a player up or a player down, as the game is designed now to leave teams often without 11 players on the field.

In conclusion, I have always been a flat back four coach but as I have developed my philosophies of playing I now realize I want my teams and players to play an aesthetically beautiful game. I am NOT obsessed with winning, though want to win more than anyone. But I want to win the RIGHT WAY, developing players to play as pure a game as possible. Playing with a back zonal three is alien in many ways to how I have taught previously, but it opens up new horizons for me and hopefully for you to consider. I am not mainstream in any shape or form in terms of my beliefs on the game. I like to think I am a forward thinker, always asking questions of myself and challenging the way the game is played.

Some of the practices in this book are not exclusive to this system of play and can be applied to others. I have added them due to what I believe is their importance in teaching the game. One example of this is "Developing Play in the Attacking Third" and then inside the penalty area and 6 yard box. Thank you for buying this book and having the interest to seek a different way to teach our wonderful game.

The 5 Phases of play in the 3-3-1-3 (3-4-3 / 3-1-3-3)

The players in our system of play

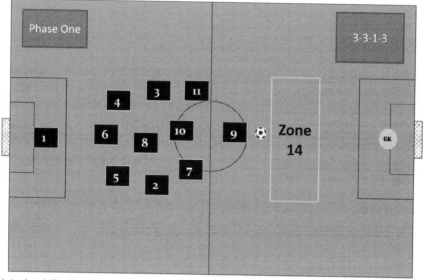

This is the defending team shape (defending start position) of a 3-3-1-3. The positioning of the wing fullbacks defensively is somewhat alien to most set ups in other formations and you have to explain and show in detail to your players how this works and why.

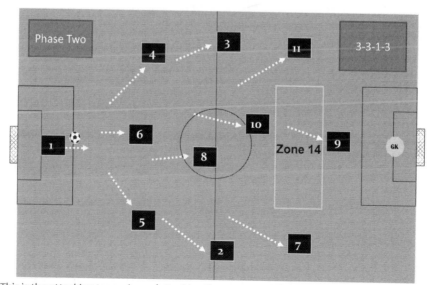

This is the attacking team shape (attacking "start position") for a 3-3-1-3. Zone 14 is the area between the opponent's back three or four and their midfield.

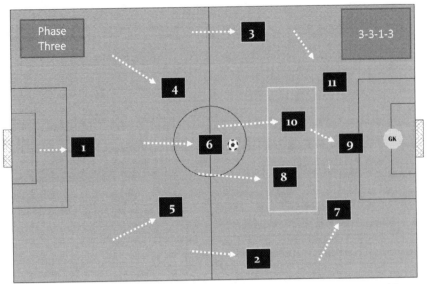

This is the attacking team shape, now possibly a 2-3-2-3 depending on the moment. This can also be the attacking team shape we change to when we are chasing a game - perhaps losing 1-0 and wanting to be more positive in attack. So this now would be the start position.

Changing team shape if we lose the ball from this attacking set up

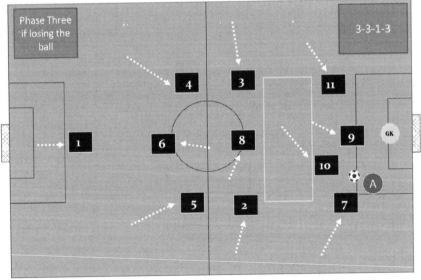

Let's say we passed the ball forward and lost it on the edge of the opponent's penalty area. Immediately, both fullbacks tuck inside to offer to fill central spaces and overload the area. (7) presses INSIDE towards (9) and (10).

Forcing the ball inside to our strength in numbers

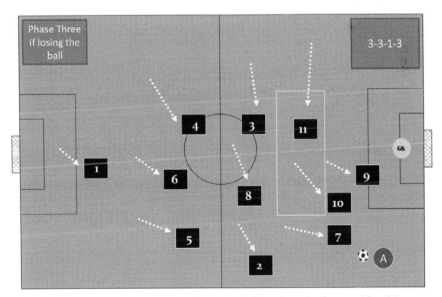

Even in a wide position, based on the pressing player (7) showing the ball inside, both wing fullbacks tuck inside because the ball is being forced into the central areas.

Forcing the ball wide and adjustment of defenders

(7) cannot get positioned quickly enough to force the ball inside, so he forces wide. This means some adjustment behind him for the right wing fullback and the right center back especially.

Interchange and Rotation

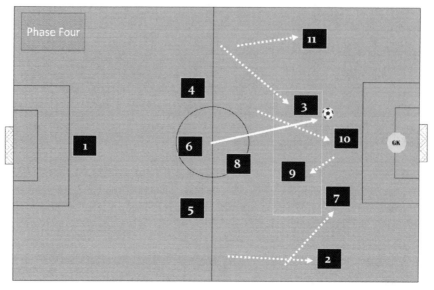

Movements up front have been affected, creating a diamond of support for striker (9) who becomes (10) and so on. These movements will be described in much more detail later.

Potential interchange movements

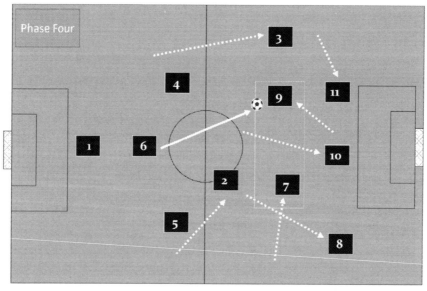

Great rotation between players should cause a lot of confusion in the opponent's defending set up. We can establish some set routines initially using a situation to set it off (6 gets the ball to feet with time, for example). Like a set play in open play to teach the players simply.

A preferred Phase Five when losing the ball: A Full Team Press

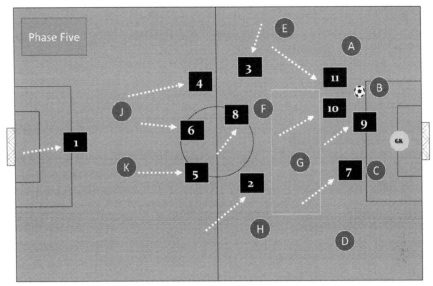

We may press up from the back too, leaving opponents offside should they get a chance of a counter attack. Defenders must decide in a split second which course of action they take.

Defensive team recovery

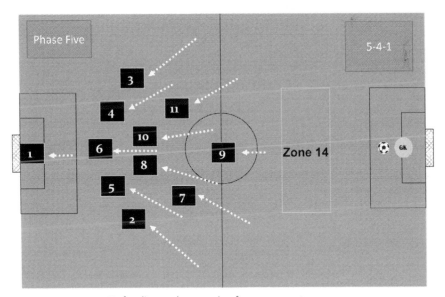

Defending and recovering from a 3-3-1-3 to a 5-4-1

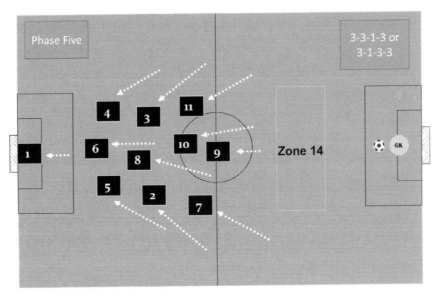

Defending and recovering to a 3-3-1-3 or 3-1-3-3

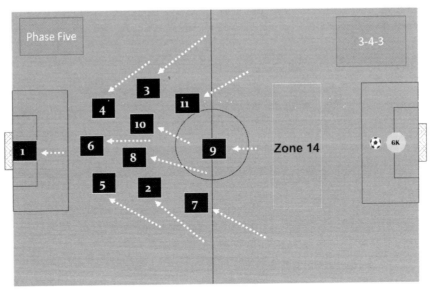

Defending and recovering to a 3-4-3

Individual Roles and Responsibilities
in the 3-3-1-3 (3-4-3 / 3-1-3-3)

Potential choices of movement in a 3-3-1-3

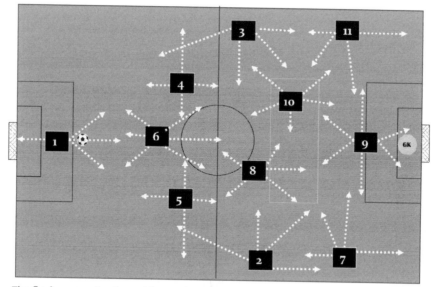

The final progression from this was the interchange of players. (8) may switch with (7), (9) with (11) and so on.

How they Link

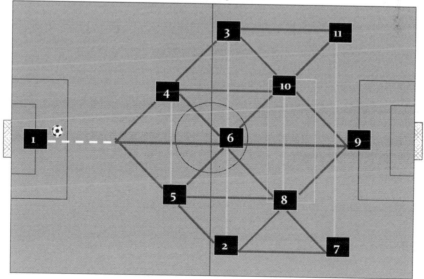

We are trying to create triangles and diamonds of support so players can set up side on to each other. It should enable many options of support. Here the team shape becomes a 2-3-2-3.

The players in our system: Passing lines of the keeper in a 3-3-1-3

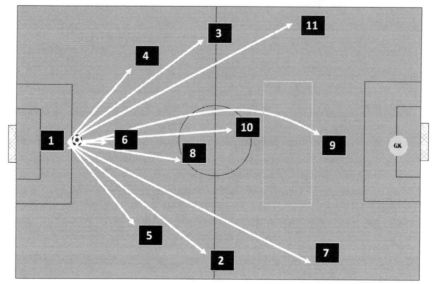

For distribution it has to be Neuer of Bayern Munich as a prime example and also Loris of Tottenham.

Keeper

Technical Qualities: In Possession
1. Speed and quality of distribution
2. Pass, kick, without hands and excellent on the floor technique.
3. Technique of releasing the ball with the feet and hands -distance (short, middle and long) with speed and direction.

Tactical: In Possession:
1. Speed -with ball TO START ATTACKS
2. Positioning -in a position to receive the back pass.
3. Choice -playing in depth -retaining possession of the ball

Out of Possession:
1. Positioning: depending on where the ball is and who has it
2. Communication -with their peers and with respect to the opponents
3. Control of ways to defend -the goal -area (at the sides, in front of the back four and behind the back four)

Psychological:
1. The "Will" to avoid goals against
2. Disciplined and responsible
3. Stable / consistent performances -avoiding risk
4. A Leader and organizer
5. Highly Vocal Communication Skills -with defenders (especially) -with the midfielders -with the forwards (can see the WHOLE FIELD)

Physical Attributes:
1. Speed over short and middle distances
2. QUICK Reactions (not anticipation)
3. Vertical Force -strong jumping ability -to attack the ball AT ITS HIGHEST POINT
4. Duel -in the air -power in the 1 to 1; so a strong body
5. Power: In kicking long, in passing.

Skill:
"The term skill refers to an ability to select and implement an appropriate and effective response from a range of possibilities. In other words, a skilled player knows what to do; when; where; how and why to do it. In other words, SKILL is 100% associated with decision making, probably THE most important part of a player's makeup.
1. Ability to recognize situations in advance of the ball
2. Ability to make correct offensive decisions in advance of the ball
3. Knowing when, where, how and why to make the best offensive decisions but BEFORE receiving the ball; not after; when its often too late.

The role of the #6 in a 3-3-1-3

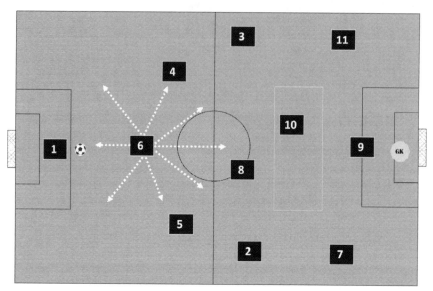

Potentially the most important pivot player on the team. Has to have many qualities; particularly to play one touch in tight areas. Traditionally (10) is the play maker, but it can also be (6) if you have the right player to do it. Liken to Buschets of Barca or Alonso of Real Madrid; or the original; Makélelé of Chelsea.

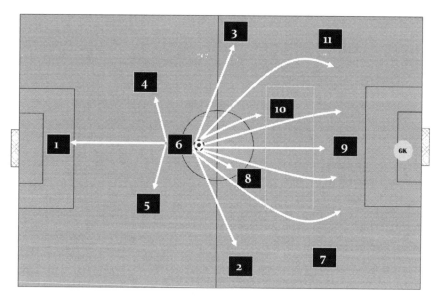

Number (6) must be able to play as a sweeper in front of the back three when we have possession and also behind the two central defenders when we lose it.

Number 6
In Possession / Without Possession
1. Technical
2. Tactical
3. Psychological
4. Physical

The number (6) is a vital player in the modern game; and the team often takes its shape around (6). In the 3-3-1-3 the 6 plays behind the center backs but often will bring the ball out and play in front.

Technical Attributes:
1. Excellent first touch control: A Great passer -short medium and long passing, ability to play ONE TOUCH.
2. Speed of play with the ball in all disciplines
3. Heading ability

Tactical Attributes:
In Possession
1. Control at speed in tight situations; so a great first touch always moving the ball quickly when able..
2. Always in a position to receive the ball and always WANTING the ball.
3. Choice –preservation of the ball -change the direction of the game.
4. Direct quick passing. Create and save the space and distance
5. Acting as a first, second or 3rd player if needed in the build up (when joining the attack)

Out of Possession
1. Orientation (Positioning according to the positioning of opponents; the ball and teammates)
2. Communication -with their peers and with respect to the opponents, particularly those immediately close, center backs, central midfielders and wing fullbacks (a position on the field of great responsibility for communication)
3. Insight in when and where to apply pressure on the ball.
4. Control of the different types of defending-between the lines, zoning, man marking, covering passing lanes

Psychological
1. Vocal leader and organizer
2. Control over the pressure of the ball.
3. Disciplined and responsible - always in a position to receive the ball first safe place to pass to.
4. Self-confidence
5. Authority
6. Charisma
7. Security for all the actions
8. Composure

Physical
1. Speed -in short and medium distances.
2. Change of pace - ability to play at three different speeds.
3. Strength of shooting and passing
4. Coordination with and without the ball
5. Agility
6. Power in the defensive 1 v 1 duel
7. Strength in the air

Skill:
1. Ability to recognize situations in advance of the ball
2. Ability to make correct decisions in advance of the ball
3. Knowing when, where, how and why to make the best decisions but BEFORE receiving the ball; not after; when its often too late.

The roles of #4 and #5

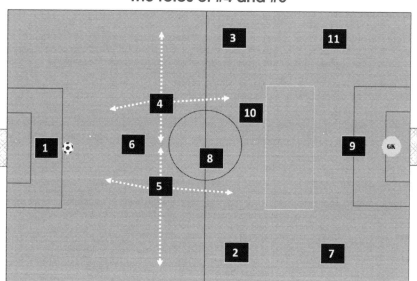

Looking for discipline in movement here but if you have the players to do it in these positions the central defender can bring the ball out of the back and (6) can fill in for him. Liken to Pique of Barcelona bringing the ball out, or Pepe of Real Madrid more defensively solid.

Numbers 4 and 5
Technical Qualities:
1. Control of the ball –excellent first touch control.
2. Heading skills.
3. Passing Technique -distance (short, medium and long) -direction (left and right)
4. Ability to play 1 touch

Tactical Qualities: In Possession
1. Speed -with the ball
2. Always in a position to receive the ball.
3. Simple Choices-first pass -retain possession of the ball – ability to change the direction of the game

Out of Possession
1. Orientation: (positioning determined by the ball, the opponent, and teammates)
2. Communication -with their peers (especially as a center back pairing)
3. Understanding of the different forms of defending; zoning and man marking; 1 v 1
4. Knowing When to press / when to cover

Psychological
1. Killer mentality (Take no prisoners).
2. Vocal leader and organizer
3. Disciplined and Responsible ensuring the first pass is a safe one; always in a position to receive (confident) -orientation -preserving the position –great positional sense.
4. Ability to focus on man marking and stick to the task if playing that style (1 to 1 and 1 more)

Physical Attributes
1. Speed in short and medium distances
2. Strength on and off the ball
3. Jumping ability
4. Strength in the challenge: On the ground: In the air.
5. Agility

The players in our system: Passing lines of #4 and #5

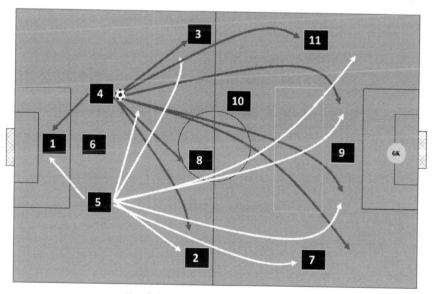

Simplicity in possession is the key here

The roles of #2 and #3

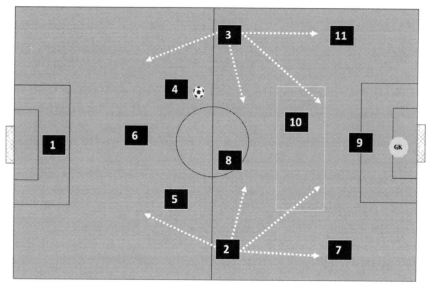

The fullbacks have incredible FREEDOM of movement in this system of play. They can become out and out wingers; or even inside right and inside left in an attacking sense. (6) assesses their positions and acts accordingly as cover. Liken to Dani Alves of Barca and Marcelo of Real Madrid. They also can tuck in defensively in front of the back three to form a defensive midfield with (8) and (10) as shown later

Numbers 2 and 3:
Technical Qualities:
1. Ability to play at speed with the ball
2. Control of the ball –excellent first touch control.
3. Technique of the pass -short, medium and long distance
4. Crossing Technique
5. Ability to play one touch

Tactical Qualities:
In Possession
1. Speed control -With the ball
2. Decision making - when to pass, run with the ball, cross, dribble, shoot and so on
3. Positioning - Always in position to receive the ball, and having a desire to receive

Out of Possession
1. Orientation: (positioning determined by the ball, the opponent, and teammates).
2. Communication - with teammates with respect of the opponents, particularly with those players always around them: closest center back, wide midfield player in front and central midfield alongside (so, 2, 4, 7 and 8). If recovering to a 3-3-1-3 shape then (2) and (3) tuck in either side of (8) in the second line of defense.
3. Understanding of the different forms of defending; zoning and man marking; 1 v 1.

Psychological
1. Disciplined and responsible -always with an attitude to receive the ball -first pass without risks –maintaining possession
2. Willingness to work for the team -in attack -defense
3. Understanding -when and where to attack; as a wing fullback with defensive duties he / she must have good decision making on this.

Physical
1. Speed -In short, medium and long distance
2. Great endurance / stamina –covering the whole of the flank
3. Strength of passing / crossing
4. Strong in the tackle / in the air
5. Agility

Skill:
1. Ability to recognize situations in advance of the ball
2. Ability to make correct decisions in advance of the ball
3. Knowing when, where, how and why to make the best decisions but BEFORE receiving the ball; not after; when its often too late.

The players in our system: Passing lines of #2 and #3

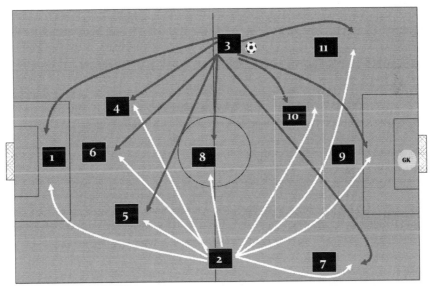

Lots of freedom of movement between players and units here highlighting those of the two fullbacks.

The roles of #8 and #10

They can interchange with various players but especially (10) patrols around Zone 14.
For 10 liken to Iniesta of Barcelona; Ozil of Arsenal or Matic of Chelsea; but with rotation.
For (8) liken to Scholes (the best historically) or Xavi of Barca.

Numbers 8 and 10

Player (8) plays differently to (10). (8) is more the link player between (6) and (10), in front of the back three. (8) is more the passer, while (10) is the more offensive creative player. They may interchange depending on the team methodology of play.

Technical:
1. Speed with the ball
2. Control of the ball –excellent first touch
3. Passing Ability -short, medium and long distance
4. Dribbling Ability -to create a 2 v 1 situation to score goals
5. Long distance shooting on goal
6. Heading Ability
7. Ability to play one touch

Tactical:
In Possession
1. Change of pace -be able to play at 3 different speeds.
2. When and where to pass (very important as they will have the ball a lot)
3. Coordination with the ball
4. Game head –when and where to move –making third man runs, can move inside to attack the goal centrally also

Out of Possession
1. Orientation (Ability to read movement off the ball)
2. Communication -with their peers and with respect to the opponent. Acumen to pressure as team
3. Control of the different types of marking -between the lines, 1 v 1 pressing

Psychological
1. Quick thinker
2. Disciplined and responsible -always in the position of receiving the ball
3. Assessing options before receiving the ball. First check -First pass
4. Orientation: Movement off the ball recognition
5. Will work for the team on offense and on defense
6. Has confidence to go deeper, to score goals, to return to the set position, to defend.

Physical
1. Speed -In short (especially), medium and long distance
2. Change of pace -be able to play at 3 different speeds.
3. Good coordination and balance with and without the ball
4. Strength of passing
5. Shooting power
6. Endurance / stamina

Skill:
1. Ability to recognize situations in advance of the ball
2. Ability to make correct decisions in advance of the ball
3. Knowing when, where, how and why to make the best decisions but BEFORE receiving the ball; not after; when its often too late.

The players in our system: Passing lines of 8 and 10

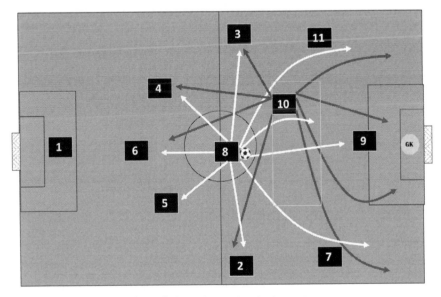

(8) and (10) are the engines in the system.

The roles of #7 and #11

Less traditional use of wide players. Often a right footer on the left and a left footer on the right can be used so they come inside to attack and shoot on goal. Liken to Messi and Ronaldo and Silva of Manchester City. (7) and (11) can be said to play inside right and inside left as support for the central striker so we become a three striker set up.

Numbers 7 and 11
Technical:
1. Speed with the ball
2. Control of the ball -first control –great first touch
3. Crossing Ability –cross with pace: on the ground or by air, with a curve out of the reach of the goalkeeper and between the goalkeeper and defenders. Where to Cross can depend on the position of goalkeeper, defenders and attackers (to the near post, to the far post, the pull back, beyond the far post). Also dribbling inside and outside to shoot at goal or to cross.
4. Passing ability
5. Scoring -balls on the floor -balls in the air

Tactical:
In Possession
1. With ball -speed control with the ball
2. Positioning-always in a position to receive, open stance, and facing towards the goal, and as open as possible
3. Know when and where to: Cross, 1 v 1 dribble, pass, or shoot.
4. Understanding of when and where to break outside to inside.

Out of Possession
1. Orientation: Movement off the ball -to attack -to defend
2. Communication -with their peers and with respect to the opponent
3. Acumen to close spaces as team
4. Ability to press and hold the position.

Psychological
1. Disciplined and responsible -make the field as large (and deep) as possible
2. Orientation. Will work for the team -on offense -on defense: close spaces and prevent deep passes
3. Confidence -Create actions for goals -Passing and crossing

Physical
1. Speed -in short, medium and long distance -technical in speed (with great coordination)
2. Endurance
3. Change of pace -be able to play at three different speeds.
4. Ability in Passing and Crossing; Dribbling; Shooting ability; Heading Ability.
5. Agility

Skill:
1. Ability to recognize situations in advance of the ball
2. Ability to make correct decisions in advance of the ball
3. Knowing when, where, how and why to make the best decisions but BEFORE receiving the ball; not after; when its often too late.

Working with (2) and (3)
Having a good understanding with the wing fullbacks as they interchange and fill in for each other.

The players in our system: Passing lines of #7 and #11

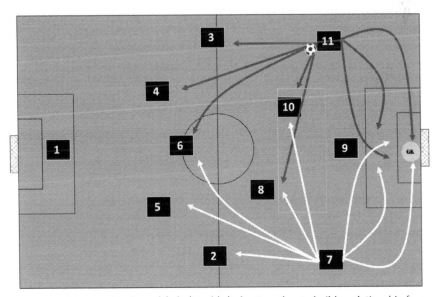

A thought to add, in training have (3), (10) and (11) play together to build a relationship for 11 v 11 even in 3 v 3 small sided games. Or (3), (4) and (6), or (8), (9) and (10), and so on.

#6 becomes a sweeper in front

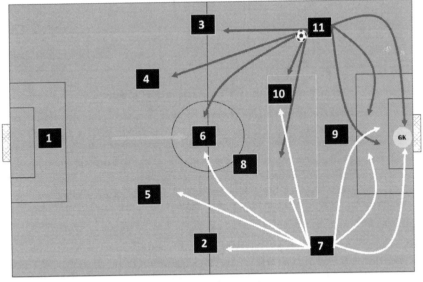

(6) is a play maker now and can bring the ball out and start the attack.

Movement Off the Ball: Interactions of #2 and #7, and #3 and #11

These relationships are vital components to the game plan in a 3-3-1-3 (or 3-1-3-3).

We want 7 and 11 to cut inside to do two things:

1. To get in a good position to receive the ball
2. To create space for overlapping Wing Full Backs 2 or 3.

Timing this movement correctly is vital, players must not come inside too soon and be easily marked. The resulting position is a player facing BACK to the ball.

This movement has to be LATE and FAST. The correct resulting positioning will be shown in these following diagrams.

Alternatively 2 and 3 can cut inside and 7 and 11 stay wide.

The timing will show that staying touchline wide will affect the opposing fullbacks' position, drawing them wider and creating more space between themselves and their center backs; which is the space we want to attack.

If the timing of the run and pass are correct; 7 or 11 will receive the ball facing FORWARD not back and be running at the defenders at pace with the ball in front of them.

Current Movements: It's all about TIMING

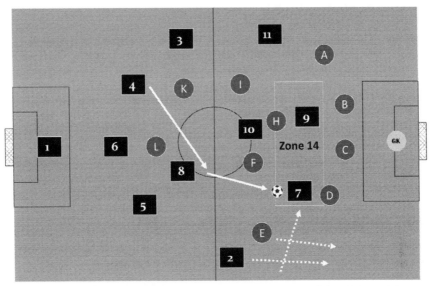

(7) has cut inside FAR TOO early to receive the pass and takes fullback (D) with them. (8) passes the ball to (7) who has to receive with his back to the defender (D) facing backwards. (E) tracks (2). We still have possession but it could be better.

Getting in too early

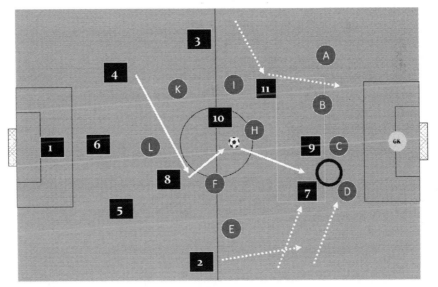

(7) in far too early; the SPACE to pass into is too tight. That said, maybe we can get (2) in because of it.

Preferred Movements: TIMING

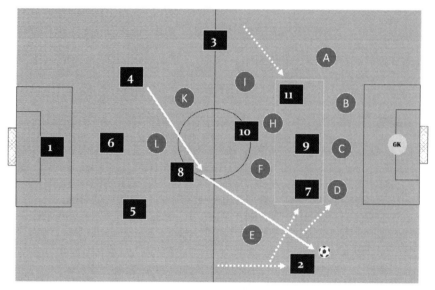

Lets say (D) reads it well and tracks (7) and closes up the space, we may still get (2) in who runs into the space left by (7)s run.. Again, TIMING is the key. As (7) moves inside this is the CUE for (2) to overlap at the same time, both LATE and FAST. We won't always catch (E) like this but if (E) is ball watching then (2) may get in on their blind side.

Preferred Movements

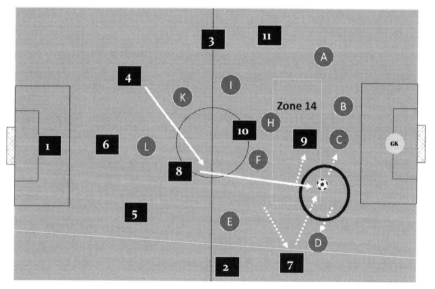

As the ball is traveling (7) moves wide and draws (D) slightly wider; creating space inside between (D) and (C). (D) IS STILL marking SPACE INSIDE; but may slide across as shown whilst hopefully (9)'s position will keep (C) away. (9) must stay out of that space or even move AWAY from it.

Alternative and unexpected

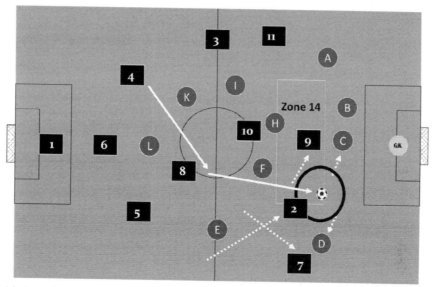

(7) clears the space inside and wing full back (2) makes the outside to inside run and has a shooting chance on goal.

Preferred Movements

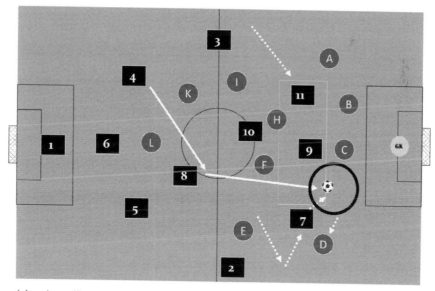

Here (7) makes a "late and fast" outside to inside run hopefully catching (D) off guard to receive the ball at pace facing forward to attack the goal. This is a far better situation than the previous one when (7) moved inside too early.

Creating 2 v 1s in vital areas outside the box across the opponent's back four

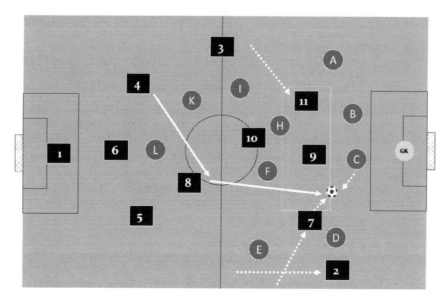

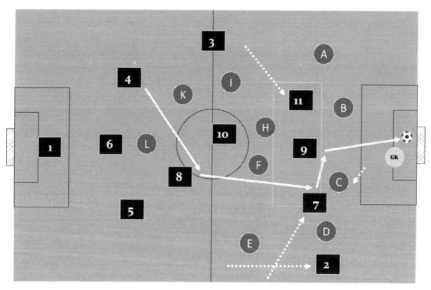

Now we have an active 2 v 1 against (D) thru (2) and (7). (7) and (9) have an active 2 v 1 against central defender (C). (11) comes inside and (A) doesn't track inside, worried about (3); so (9) and (11) have an active 2 v 1 situation against central defender (B).

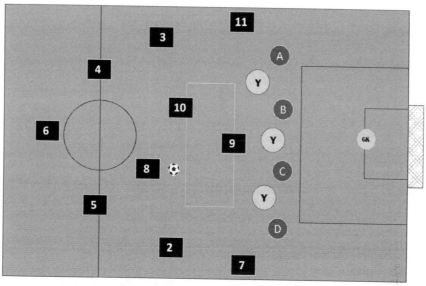

Spaces we are trying to exploit in yellow(Y) and between defenders. What we do will depend on how the opponents position and defend.

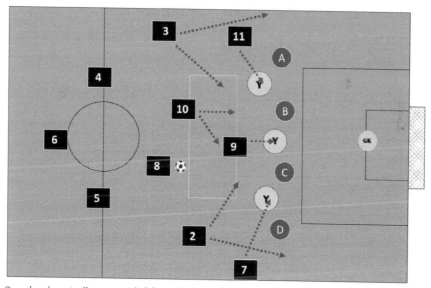

Over-load centrally now with (7) and (11) attacking the inside spaces between defenders. Fullbacks can attack inside or stay wide to effect the positioning of (A) and (D).

Cutting inside to attack the central spaces

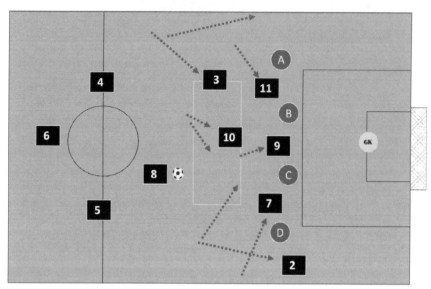

2 v 1s created across the back four. Of course opponent midfield players will track back but if this is well rehearsed by us in training we may catch them by surprise in the game and their reactions may be too late to stop it. Even bigger overloads when (2), (3) and (10) join in.

Interchanges of Attackers

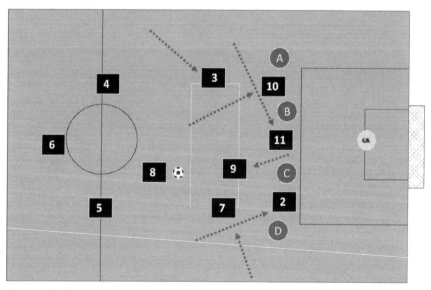

Interchanges of players now. I am leaving the back four intact here; but likely defenders may track opponents and leave spaces open. What will (D) do with (2) or (7)? Will (B) and (C) go short with (9), leaving a big space centrally?

Exploiting a central space created by off the ball movement by #9

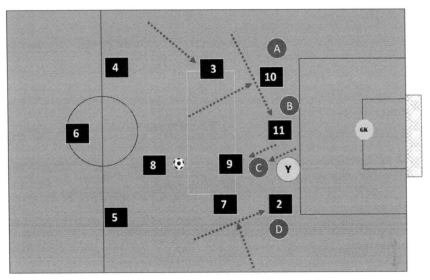

Just one defender (Y) tracking one player; in this case (C) tracking (9) short; will create a central gap for (11) or (2). If (C) doesnt track (9) then (9) can receive to feet side on; turn; and attack in a 2 v 1 with either (2) or (11) against (C).

Another idea

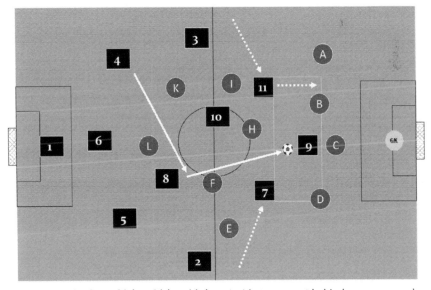

As an example: Into the feet of (9) and (7) and (11) cut inside to support behind or one can make a run in front for the next phase of play. (8) into (9) who lays off to (7) who plays it forward to (11).

More ideas

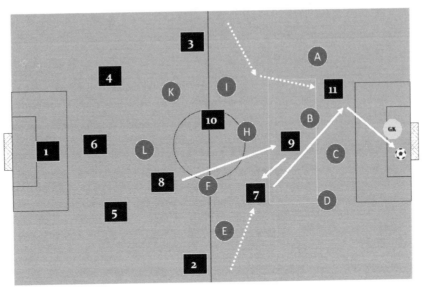

End Product, a Third Man Run from (11)

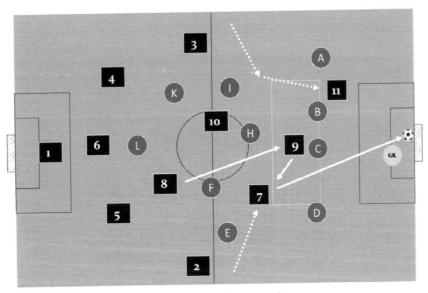

End Product, a shot on goal

The role of #9

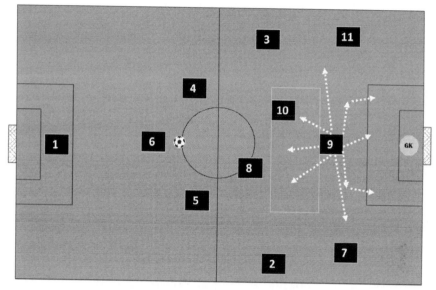

Target man, or play running channels (or both). Able to interchange positions and have great mobility but in and around zone 14 and the width of the penalty area generally.
Liken to Robin Van Persie and Karim Benzema.

Number 9
Technical
1. Speed with the ball
2. Control of the ball -first control –great first touch in all directions-Ability to keep the ball dribbling ability
3. Ability to play Give and go's-pass to the side (left and right) -cut pass (chip)
4. Passing ability
5. Shooting and heading ability
6. Ability to play one touch

Tactical:
In Possession
1. Speed -with ball -control without the ball
2. Positioning-without ball to receive it: always in position to receive 1 v 1, in depth and always in a position to receive –
3. With the ball: choose direct / indirect play, create chances for others or retain possession of the Ball

Out of Possession
1. Orientation (Creative movement without the ball)
2. Communication -with their peers and with respect to the opponents
3. Acumen to pressure as a team player
4. Control of the different types of pressure -between the lines

Psychological
1. Killer mentality.
2. With self-confidence -(to create AND SCORE goals)
3. Disciplined and responsible
4. Willingness to work for the team -in attack –defense
5. Self belief to KEEP going back after missing chances

Physical
1. Speed -in short (especially), medium and long distance -technical in speed (Great coordination and first touch control at pace)
2. Change of pace -be able to play at THREE different speeds.
3. Ability of passing and dribbling
4. Ability in the air. Strength in 1 v 1; in the air, on the ground to keep the ball under pressure
5. Agility

Skill:
1. Ability to recognize situations in advance of the ball
2. Ability to make correct decisions in advance of the ball
3. Knowing when, where, how and why to make the best decisions but BEFORE receiving the ball; not after; when its often too late.

The players in our system: Passing lines of 9

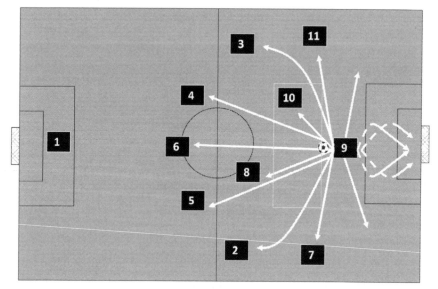

Potential passing lanes of (9).

THE RELATIONSHIP BETWEEN (7), (9) AND (11)
ATTACKING
When we attack, these three form a three pronged attack. In the 3-3-1-3 often the two wide attackers tuck in to support the central striker (9). They may do it at the same time to form a three or, depending on which side of the field the ball is on, one will tuck in to form a two pronged attack. These three may interchange to confuse the defenders. They need a good understanding of how to work as a three and also a two, and when to tuck in and when to stay wide.

Barcelona show this perfectly with the interchanges of Messi, Neymar and Suarez with no real set positions for any of them. They have the freedom to interchange and move around, which makes it very difficult for each defender to know who to pick up.

DEFENDING
The central striker (or whoever is filling that role at the time between the three strikers) must be the first line of defense. When the time is right, (7) and (11) will press as quickly as possible wherever the ball is.

THE RELATIONSHIP BETWEEN (9) AND (10)
ATTACKING
They must develop a good understanding of movement off the ball to complement each other. Interchanging of positions can cause much confusion in the opponent's defense, so they have to develop good mutual timing of this movement.

Angled positions off each other will help them in a supporting capacity.

At the same time they will link up together and form a formidable unit of two.

Generally (10) is positioned behind (9) but it can be the reverse at different moments in the game to confuse defenders.

DEFENDING
They can help each other by pressing as a unit high up the field. Better to work as a pair if it is possible with early pressing of opponents with the reward of winning the ball in an area from which they can shoot immediately on goal.

The relationship of the back three

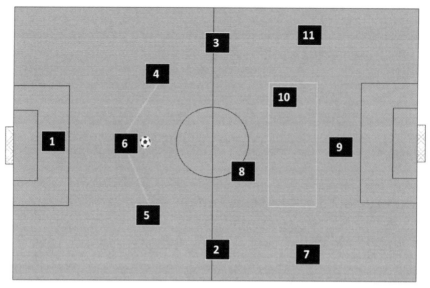

These three players defend zonally not man marking in my system of play. That's not to say another coach cant use two man markers and a sweeper but I want us to have more freedom at the back so we mark zones. Often 2 man makers means these two players aren't always free to play when in possession as they have a man marking philosophy embedded in their mind.

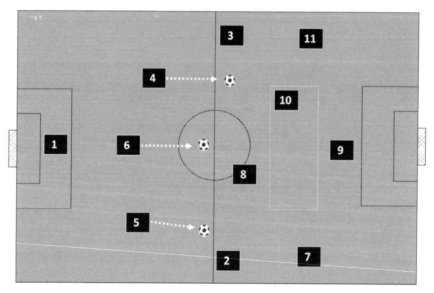

All three players in my set up MUST be able to play from the back and be ultra comfortable on the ball. Here we show all three on a ball and they are encouraged to join in or instigate the attack. Whichever one does we will have a player to cover for him so he knows he is allowed this freedom with security behind him.

An example of attacking from the back and covering

The simplest of rotations but (6) has the confidence to bring the ball out if there is space to run into knowing (8) will drop in and cover.

Another example

(5) brings the ball out this time and (8) covers again. It could be (6) covers across and (8) drops to (6) or even (2) dropping back in to cover, but if opponents have two up front we must make sure we don't leave 2 v 2 at the back.

Opponents push three up to create a 3 v 3

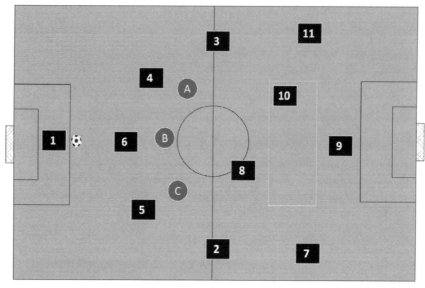

This is something to look for and guard against. Personally, I don't want to leave us with a 3 v 3 so we can drop (8) back (if (8) is capable) to make it a back four OR push (6) into defensive midfield and drop the wing backs deeper to form a back four with the remaining two center backs.

We change formation to a 4-2-3-1

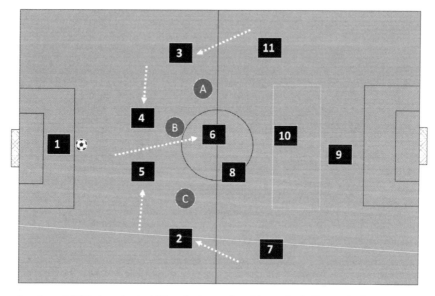

In this system I want (6) to be a typical (6) so he is comfortable on the ball. We don't want to change our method to suit the opponents but it may be needed so we will teach the players this. Now we have a 4 v 3 in our favor but (2) and (3) should attack and try to force (A) and (C) back anyway.

Changing systems of play to suit the team

Changing systems from 3-1-3-3 to 4-2-3-1

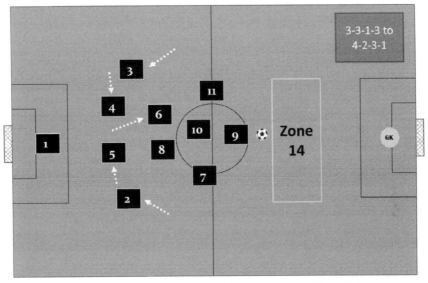

A very simple switch. (6) pushed into midfield, (2) and (3) drop back and (4) and (5) come closer together

Changing systems from 3-3-1-3 to 3-2-2-3

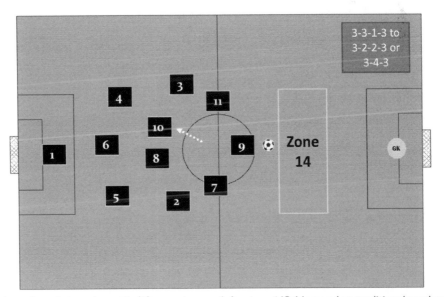

(10) drops in and plays alongside (8) so we have 4 defensive midfielders and no traditional number (10)
We are now making the center stronger in front of the back three.

Attacking team shape of the 3-2-2-3

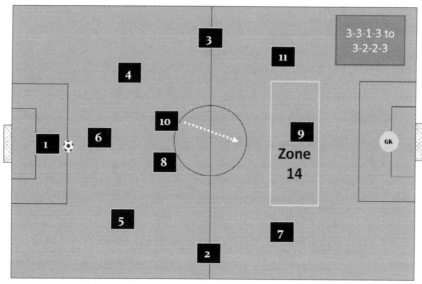

Either (8) or (10) pushes on, usually (10) because (10) will be that type of player.

Changing systems from 3-3-1-3 to 3-2-3-2

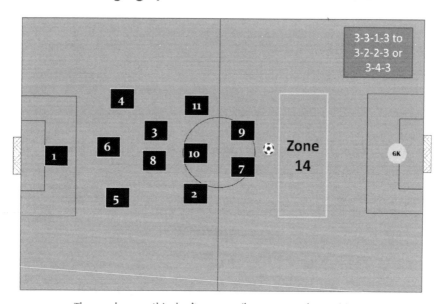

The numbers on this don't necessarily represent the positions.

Opponents play with only one up

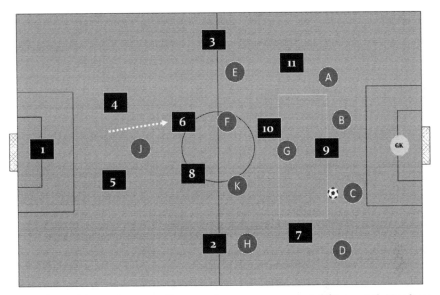

We don't need three players marking one player, so we can push (6) into midfield in front of the two center backs (4) and (5). Opponents set up in a 4-1-4-1 here for example. Now our shape is more a 2-4-1-3. It could be 4 or 5 instead of 6 depending on who is best suited to move up into midfield.

Defensive Positioning

To play such a fluid and imaginative style of play, where players are offered such freedom offensively all over the field, there are always weaknesses exposed which we need to address. In this case we look at the defensive consequences for which we need to cover and correct.

Pressing in the ATTACKING; MIDDLE and DEFENSIVE thirds of the field

Pressing Quickly in the ATTACKING third of the field

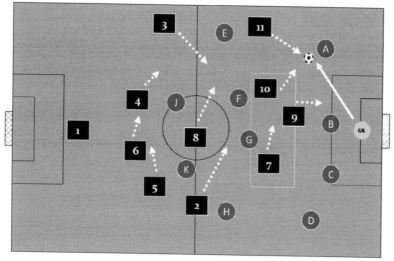

We set up to immediately force the defender (A), due to (11)'s positioning in the press, to pass INSIDE, cutting off the pass to (E) wide. This is where we are strong in numbers.

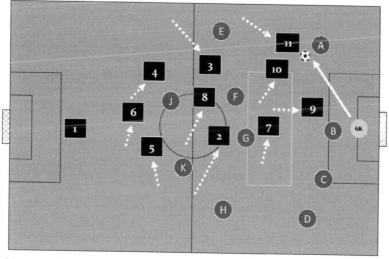

(9) covers and cuts off the back pass to the keeper. Here we have 5 lines of defense including the keeper. A 1-3-3-3-1

Pressing Quickly in the MIDDLE third of the field

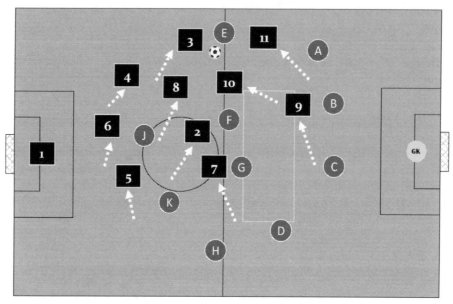

The same principle applies in the middle of the field we want to show / force the ball INSIDE because that's where our overload of players is.. We have a 3-4 behind the ball and 3 recovering back. This is quite a radical change for a wing back in terms of recovery position being more central and in a midfield area.

If (10) is able to recover back in time

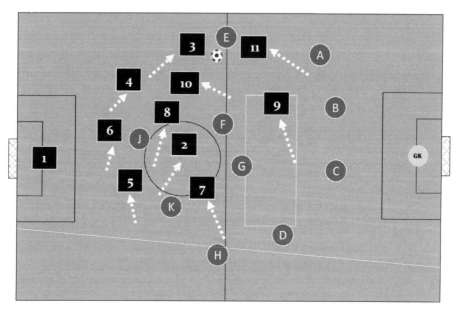

Here we see (10) helping out the defense by recovering back BEHIND the ball not in front of it as in the last diagram. This makes us even more solid behind the ball to win it back immediately, almost a 3-5-2 defensively. (11) can double team from the other side with (3).

Alternative position of (7)

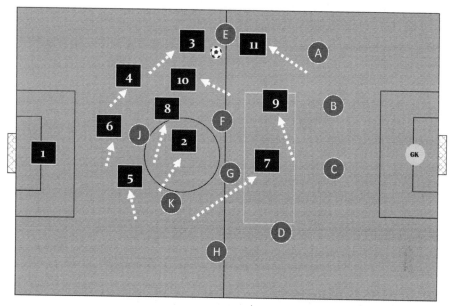

Should the ball be passed backwards by (E) then (7) can help (11) and (9) to press.

Defending in the defending third

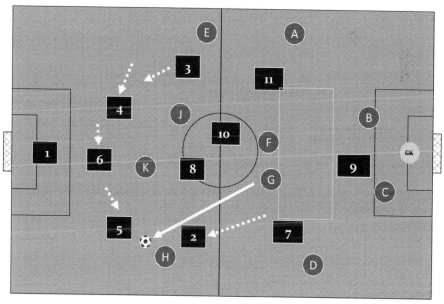

Pressurizing -Fullback (2) closes quickly as the ball travels. Shows the player inside or outside depending on where the support is, how fast and how good a defender (2) is. (7) can double up to help.

Making play predictable - For teammates to adjust their position. Close the spaces close to the ball. (8), (10) and (9) recover back. Leave the far players away from the ball.'

Support positions – Angle / Distance / Communication.

Regaining the ball – Strikers and midfield be ready to break quickly.

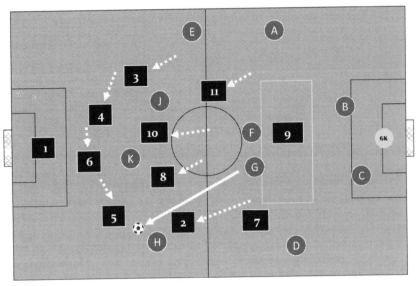

1. This is how the situation looks when the players have made their movements.
2. Observe how the defending team have compacted as a team in terms of width and length on the field.
3. They have filled the spaces close to the ball reducing the room to play in. (3) and (11) who have moved across the field remain focused on the fact that they are responsible for (A) and (E) respectively should the play switch to the other side of the field hence their body stances are open so they can see both the ball and their immediate opponents.

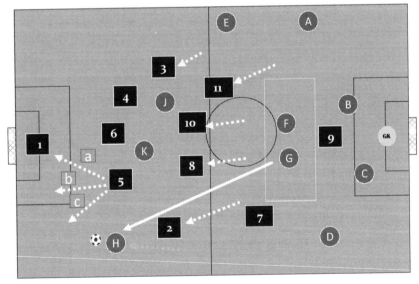

1. The opponents have got behind our team in a wide area. (5) has three choices:
   a) Can I tackle ?
   b) Can I stop the cross by getting in the line of it ?
   c) Do I recover to the goal ?
2. Depends how close to the crosser (5) is, if too far away then work back to goal because the danger isn't where the ball is coming from; but where it is going to.
3. (4), (5) and (6) should recover back to mark the danger zones in the box and will mark players who enter those zones.
4. Marking the near post, mid goal and the far post areas. (8) (10) and (11) recover to zones in and around the box for pull backs.

Poor positioning from the cross cost us this goal

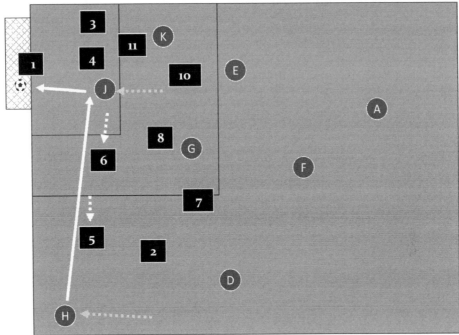

1. Center back (6) also gets pulled out of position and (J) is left free at the near post to score.
2. (5), (6) and (4) should mark zones in the box. They attack the areas in front of them and don't drop back on top of their team mates. The same applies to (8) and (11). (3) also has to cover the areas behind them if the ball is hit very long.
3. They pick up players who enter their zones. (5) must resist the temptation to go towards (H) to try to stop the cross from so far away the danger is in the box not where the ball is coming from, by the time (5) gets close the cross has gone in perhaps to the gap where (5) came from and the opposition striker (J) has a free strike on goal. (6), (4) and (3) can fill in but we need to avoid too much adjustment.
4. If we win a header the clearance should be high, wide and long. The defense should push up quickly to the edge of the box and beyond if possible (depends on distance of the headed clearance, who the ball goes to and what direction it
5. (6) Is out of position, center back (5) closes down but cannot affect the cross.

What should have happened

The danger is at the near post, not at the crosser, so center back (5) stays in position and covers the near post and clears the ball.

1. (5), (6) and (4) mark zones. They attack the areas in front of them and don't drop back on top of their teammates. The same applies to (3), (8), (10) and (11). (3) and (4) also have to cover the areas behind them if the ball is hit very long. They pick up players who enter their zones.
2. (5) must resist the temptation to go towards (H) to try to stop the cross. The danger is in the box, not where the ball is coming from. By the time (5) could get close enough to affect (H), the cross will likely have already gone in, perhaps to the gap left by (5), and the opposition have a free strike on goal. (6), (4) and (3) can fill in but we need to avoid too much adjustment.
3. If they win a header, the clearance should be high, wide and long. The defense should push up quickly to the edge of the box and beyond if possible (this depends on the distance of the headed clearance, who the ball goes to and in what direction).

What could also have happened

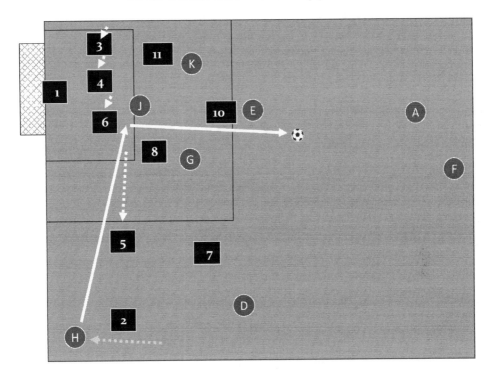

1. The center back does close, leaving the near post free, but (6) moves into that important space and covers it and is able to clear with a header.
2. So now (6), (4) and (3) mark zones. They each have changed positons and moved one position forward. (11) can drop in behind (3) if needed. They attack the areas in front of them and don't drop back on top of their teammates.
3. They pick up players who enter their zones. (5) has made the decision to move towards (H) to try to stop the cross, which is not the best decision, as the danger is in the box, not where the ball is coming from. By the time (5) gets close, the cross has gone in. Fortunately (6) has covered just in case.
4. (6), (4) and (3) can fill in as seen here but we need to avoid too much adjustment.

Another possibility

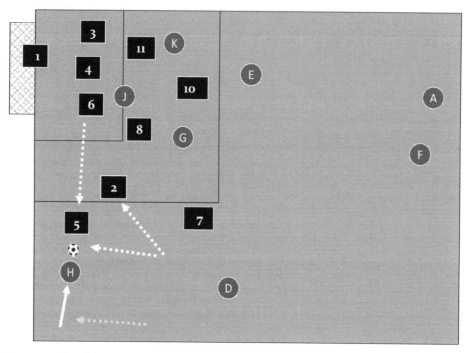

1. The center back has to close down (H) as (H) is attacking inside. (6) moves into that important space (5) has left and covers it just in case..
2. If the wide player decides to bring the ball towards goal, (5) is the closest and must close the ball down. (6), (4) and (3) move across to cover the nearest danger zones (rope theory), and (11) can drop back in to take (3)'s place if needed.
3. (2) may have recovered back into a good defensive position or he can double team (H), particularly if (5) has held up the attacker.

High Pressing as a Team

Pressing quickly after losing the ball

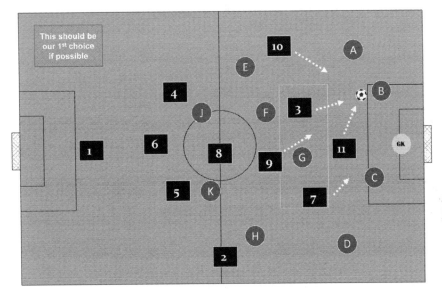

First thought is "Can we win the ball back immediately or at least within 6 seconds; and in the ATTACKING THIRD"?

Regaining possession very close to goal

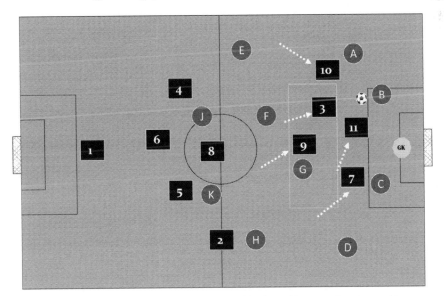

If we win the ball back here we can attack immediately and be very close to goal to score. This saves the whole team a lot of recovery energy they would otherwise need.

Focusing on the back players in our team

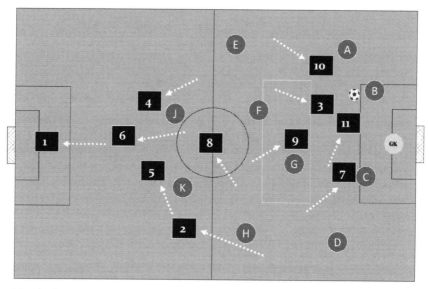

Whilst the front players attack, the back players can drop off and guard against a counter attack IN ANTICIPATION of the ball being played in behind.

Full Team Press

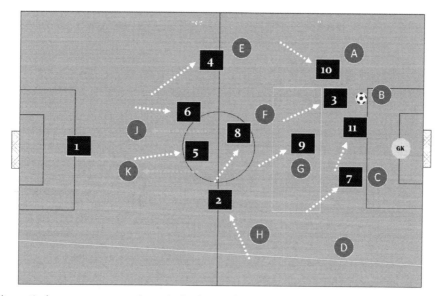

Alternatively we may press up from the back as well, leaving opponents offside should they get a chance of a counter attack. Defenders must decide in a split second which course of action they take.

A long clearance from the back to the front by the opponents

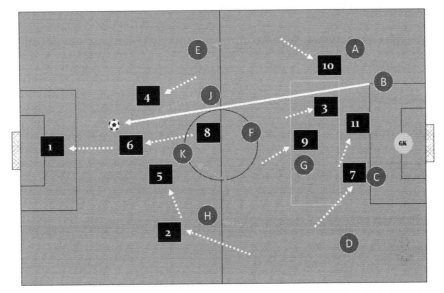

We were not able to press quickly enough to stop the delivery. They play a long clearance in behind us, we DROP quickly at the back.

Full Team Press from the back to the front

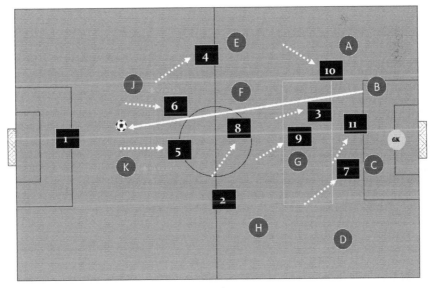

We pressed too late close to the ball to stop the delivery. So we may press up from the back too, leaving opponents offside. This shows another way to anticipate a situation.

They get the ball out and keep possession; we have to press and also recover at the same time

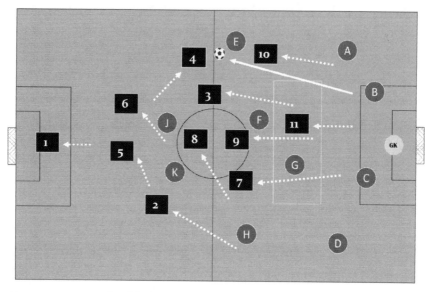

Now we must press thru (4) who MUST delay (E), and the rest of the team can then get compact behind, alongside and in front of the opponents. (3) and (10) can recover to the press also.

Defensive Readjustment When Losing the Ball

The interchange of individual players in attack initially

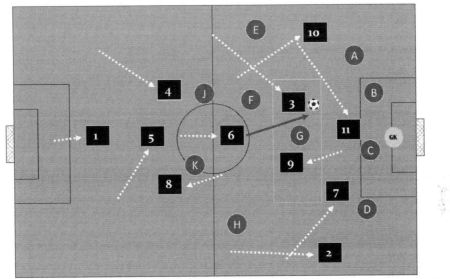

When we attack, our players have freedom of expression, which means when we lose the ball many players may be out of position defensively (as shown above). (6) passes to (3) in a central attacking position. (8) could drop centrally to cover or as shown here into a wide defensive position to cover with (5) tucking into (6)'s opposition.

We lose the ball with a bad pass after attacking rotations of players

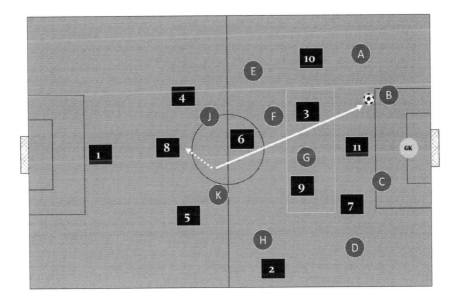

Players have interchanged positions and now we are caught having to defend. We need to immediately regain our defensive discipline.

How to teach this

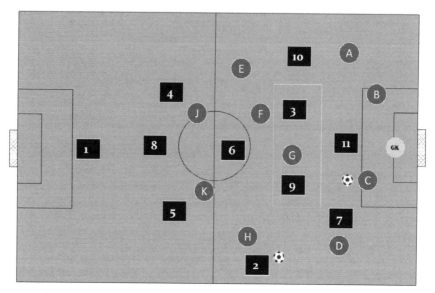

The ball is with our right wing fullback attacking. The Coach will wait until the attacking team have interchanged as so many players are in different positions on the field to their normal ones. Then the coach will throw a 2nd ball in to the opponents (to (C) here). The numbers team must forget the first ball and set up defensively against this new ball. We can't press as a team, so we retreat back; though (11) can try to press as he is closest.

The stages of development for this are as follows:

- An 11 v 11 game situation
- Go through the 5 phases of attack in a Shadow Play and make sure there is a lot of rotation and interchange so players are in quite different positions to their normal ones by the time we hit Phase 4.
- Give the ball to the opponents in a certain place, have that team stand still, have your team adjust around the ball "defensively".
- First player (11) MUST PRESS AND DELAY if possible.
- Therefore, based on the previous diagram: 11 is now 9, 9 is now 10, 6 is now 8, 8 is now 6, 10 is now 11 and 3 is inside left, an in-between position.
- They position in their new respective positions defensively and don't necessarily immediately transition back to their own positions (unless very close to them already).
- Start the play from there with opponents in possession
- Once we win it back we start the attacking rotations again
- To help teach and clarify the changing positions of players as the game is progressing, call a player's name and indicate how his position has changed.
- Example: number 10 becomes 6; number 11 becomes 8; 8 becomes 9; and so on.
- Advice and immediate feedback is required from the coach until it is clear what the purpose and result of the rotation is; both offensively and defensively.
- Even ask the players for an instant assessment of their new position as the game is going on (say his name, have him call out his new position; which can change in a moment).

- Stop it periodically for players to see it.
- Again point out the new numbered position "defensively" to clarify how it all changes.
- So: game in motion, our team has possession, throw a 2nd ball in, forget the first ball, now opponents have possession, they stand still until we get into our defensive shape (as quickly as possible, have players correct themselves if need be), then let it go live again, opponents in possession.
- Finally, once you've established the differences between attacking and defending positioning with the players, let them play a full 11 v 11 and observe if they are making the correct judgments (and making them quickly) as they transition from attacking to defending and defending to attacking
- Players must transition back to their original positions as soon as they can once a phase of play is over and a new one is beginning.
- Beware, some players just run all over the place without thought or method. We have a framework to work within.

Defensive rotational recovery positions

Due to our attacking rotations, players are often out of position defensively when we lose the ball. Here we show how players position to help each other and eventually work themselves back to their own natural positions on the team. Learning this approach and understanding how to cover for each other immediately gives the team a wonderful means of attacking freedom and expression.

We are in attacking mode: both wing fullbacks attacking

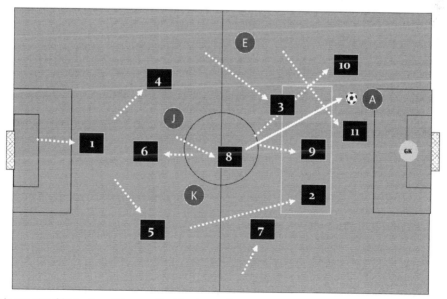

This is our attacking set up. We are attacking in numbers with players in different positions from their traditional ones because we allow freedom of rotation. Here (8) passes to (10) but the ball is intercepted by opposing player (A). For clarity, not all opponents are shown.

We attack and lose the ball

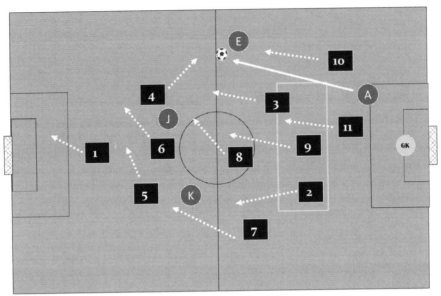

We lose the ball to player (A) who plays it forward to player (E). Now showing the start positions for the recovery and changing of positions depending on where the ball is played. This shows their positions initially and where they will move to.

We condense our defensive shape

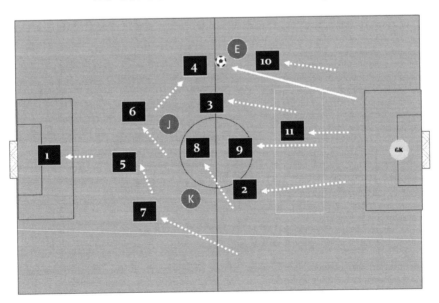

Player positioning is now different defensively but it doesn't matter as long as we can create our defensive shape. Players recover in straight lines or the shortest route back to goal, or to the ball.

How we press and recover and who does what, where and why

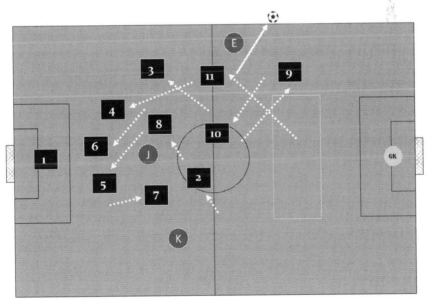

Changes: Our Center back (4) is now a left wing fullback (3); our central defender (6) is a left defender (5); our left defender (5) is a central defender (6); our left back (3) is a center midfielder, our right wing fullback (2) is a right winger (7); our right winger (7) is a right center back (5), our striker (9) is a number (10); our attacking midfielder (10) is in the wide left(11) position and our wide left (11) is in the (9) position.

Showing Players positions after rotating back to their original team shape during a break in the game

Example: The ball goes out of play and the players rotate back into their own positions.

To recap on the previous defensive recovery set up which was our offensive set up initially:

1. Our Center back (4) is now a left fullback 3;
2. Our linking midfielder (8) is a center back 4;
3. Our left back (3) is a center midfielder 8,
4. Our striker (9) is now a number 10;
5. Our attacking midfielder (10) is in the wide left position 11;
6. Our wide left striker (11) is in the (9) central striker position;
7. Our right fullback (2) is in 7s wide striker position;
8. Our wide right striker (7) is in right center back (5)s position.

The Moral of all this?

In developing and actively encouraging a team to play with incredible freedom and fluidity within the team framework set by the coach, we must also address what can go wrong defensively when playing this way.

In particular, it can leave us vulnerable to a counter attack. Through the freedom of movement, players are often out of their own positions and may feel a little lost if we lose the ball as to where they need to go next. Often, for example, a fullback will attack up and down the field, making a 50 yard run but dreading the 50 yard run back to his position if we lose the ball. If this is not addressed with the fullback, then he may be less effective offensively, as the thought of all the recovery runs may put him off. Plus it may also be too physically challenging for him over the course of a full game.

Showing players how to compensate for this, how to cover for each other, how to save energy, will encourage them to continue with their offensive style knowing they know how best to defend if they lose the ball. In this way, that PERCEIVED WEAKNESS in the system of play may in fact be transformed into a REAL STRENGTH of the team.
To make this work, though, we need a team of UNSELFISH PLAYERS PREPARED TO WORK AND HELP EACH OTHER.

Coaches should set these situations up in training to show the players who does what and when. Show the attacking shape, with many interchanges, then stop the action. Throw another ball into the opponents and then have them stand still in position, giving our team time to see how they can position defensively immediately after losing the ball. Once they can see how to do it, make it live again and let it go free.

Defensive Adjustment And Organization

The potential weakness in this system and STYLE of play is the defensive adjustments needed to ensure that our fluidity of attacking movement doesn't cost us when we lose possession of the ball.

This presentation shows how we can make sure we are disciplined and solid defensively by teaching the players where to immediately press, where and when to recover and how to fill in and cover for each other immediately after the ball is lost.

Therefore, we transition (in MIND and BODY) from incredible freedom of attacking momentum; which brings imagination, interchanges and rotations, to the opposite; intense, concentrated and positionally disciplined defense.

This is a simple way to show how we can make sure the team is well organized to allow the attacking freedom to take place, knowing we can cover ourselves if we lose the ball.

Positioning at the back when losing the ball

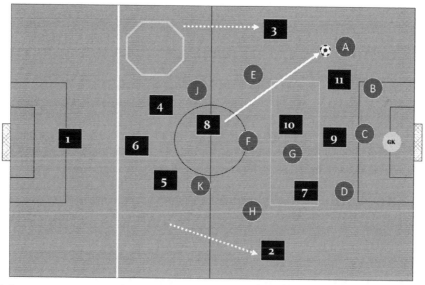

I think this is our greatest potential weakness defensively (the wide areas of the field) and we need to train the players to deal with it. Both wing backs attacking. When lose the ball, the most vulnerable place for us is the wide area on the side of the ball as shown. We mark "goal-side" and leave the wide area open.

We are exposed with a 1 v 1 wide

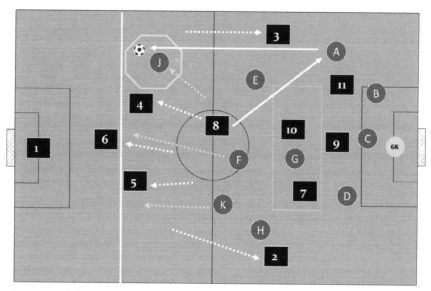

If (J) is fast we are in big trouble now as he attacks defender (4) in a 1 v 1. He could run inside to goal or into a crossing position. The next slide shows how we can prevent this before it happens.

What Should Happen

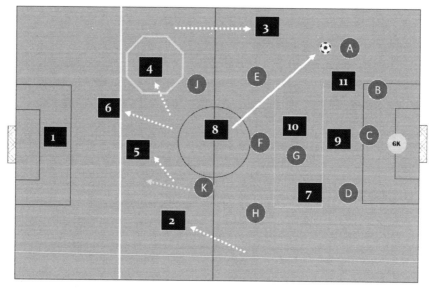

(4) moves channel side of (J) and with depth to fill the space and prevent the pass. (6) drops in to cover or (5) can do it if he is closer. This may delay the forward momentum of (A) and allow recovery runs. (4) should anticipate a giveaway. Players are USUALLY told to mark GOALSIDE; but sometimes they need to do the opposite, such as here. (4) marks (J) "Channel Side" so (4) drops off and across into the space that the ball is intended to go into. With a defending player already in there this should be enough to put off the passer from playing the ball to that area and we stop the attack before it begins.

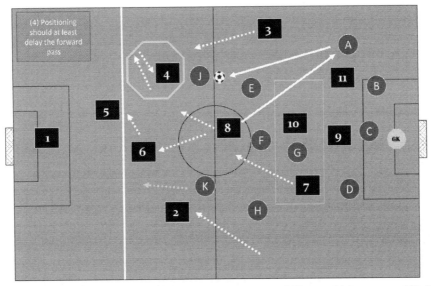

Here (5) adds cover to (4) if needed, and (6) drops back to cover (K)'s run. If (A) passes to (J)'s feet (as shown) then (4) has time to close (J) down and control the situation with (J) having his back to goal. Other players will try to recover back.

Alternatively, press up front

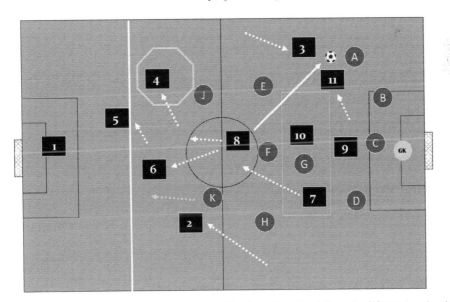

If (3) and (11) are close enough they can press immediately to stop the delivery by (A). But we should still have center back (4) fill the space down the side and (5) and (6) drop off for extra security.

Now a Full Team Press from the back three also

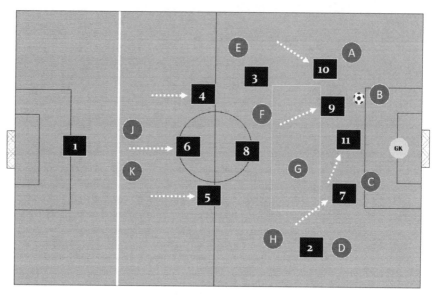

Alternatively we may press up from the back as well, leaving opponents offside should they get a chance of a counter attack. Defenders must decide in a split second which course of action they take. YOU CANNOT DO THIS TOO CLOSE TO THE HALF WAY LINE AS THERE IS TOO LITTLE MARGIN FOR ERROR AND TOO MUCH SPACE BEHIND.

We lose the ball with both wing backs attacking

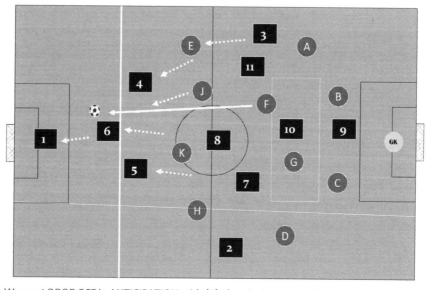

We must DROP OFF in ANTICIPATION with (6) already dropped off in a covering position.

What we shouldn't do

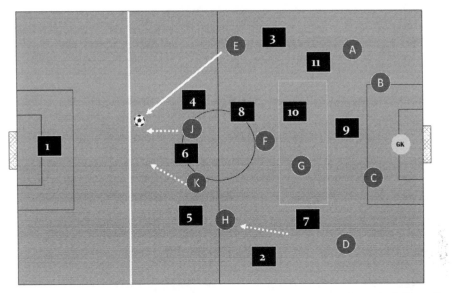

This can happen too much; we push up and are TOO FLAT AND GET CAUGHT near the half way line. We should NOT defend flat on the half way line as there is too much space in behind.

What we should do

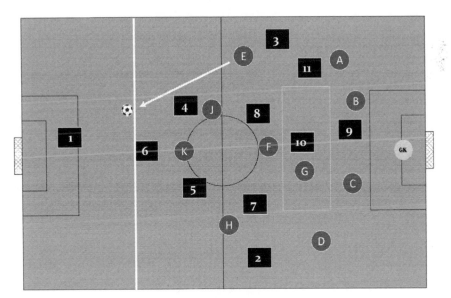

Both wing backs attacking. This is how we should be set up if no pressure on the ball to prevent the forward pass.

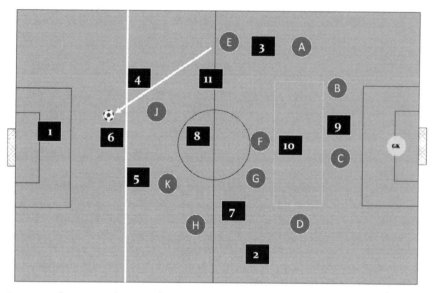

As we get closer to goal we can flatten out somewhat as there is much less space behind and the keeper can be the sweeper. So we are looking to flatten about half way to goal from the half way line.

We condense our defensive shape and HOLD the line

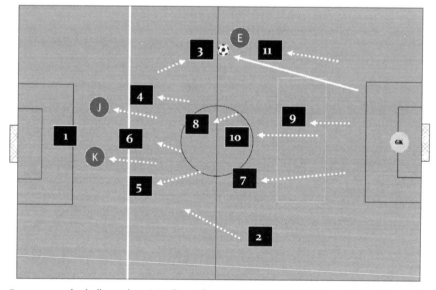

Pressure on the ball: we drop initially until we see the ball CANNOT be delivered forward. That is the time to HOLD THE LINE or STEP UP. Let opponents run offside. If we get caught at least there is less space behind to play into and the keeper may work as a sweeper.

DROP OFF and then STEP UP

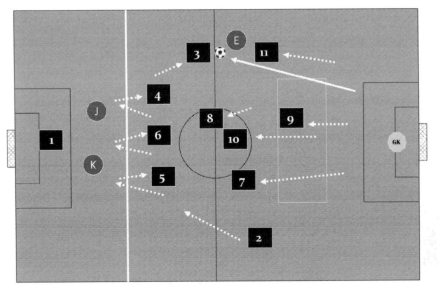

Here we DROP OFF then STEP UP as we see pressure on the ball. We leave (J) and (K) WELL OFFSIDE. This requires COMMUNICATION and ORGANIZATION.

We condense our defensive shape

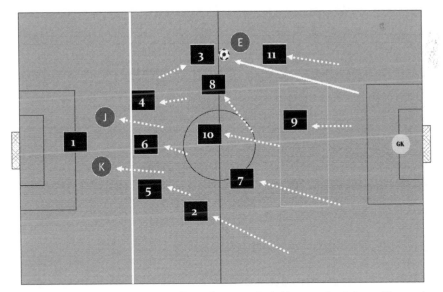

Pressure on the ball: we drop initially until we see the ball cannot be delivered forward. That is the time to HOLD THE LINE or STEP UP. Player positioning is now different defensively but it doesn't matter as long as we can create our defensive shape. Players recover in straight lines or the shortest route back to goal, or to the ball.

Defensive pressing to push up without touching the ball

This is a great session to teach the players how they can push opponents back even when THE OPPONENTS have the ball. We will try to push them back without even touching the ball ourselves. We start on the edge of our box and try to get our back three up to the half way line. Setting conditions will help us do this to start the process off.

Conditions:
1. Defending team cannot tackle.
2. Defending team CAN intercept a pass.
3. Attacking team must play 1 or 2 touches.

Coaching Points:
1. Defenders press the ball as quickly as possible.
2. Stop the forward pass, try to force a pass across the field or backwards.
3. Defenders must recognize every opportunity to push up no matter how small a distance it may be.
4. Sometimes it's 5 yards up, 3 yards back for example, depending on the position of the ball and if there is pressure.
5. Try to intercept the pass and gain possession.

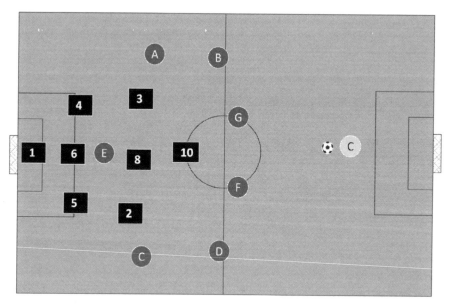

This session is teaching defenders how to push up and force the opponents back without touching the ball. The goal is to start on the edge of the box with the opponents in possession but by pressing and pushing up at the right times we force opponents back. Our aim is to get our back 3 up to the half way line. So this is moving approximately 40 yards up the field.

Start with equal numbers so success can be achieved

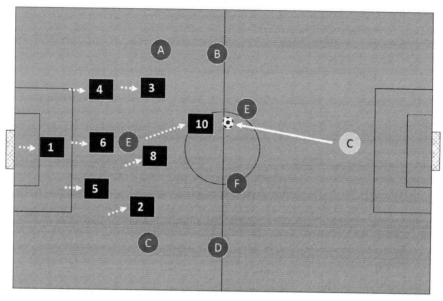

7 v 7 plus the keeper. Conditions are introduced to help the session. Coach passes to (E) and (10) presses to try to stop a forward pass. Defending team may sneak up 2 or 3 yards if (1) can delay.

Sliding up and across the field

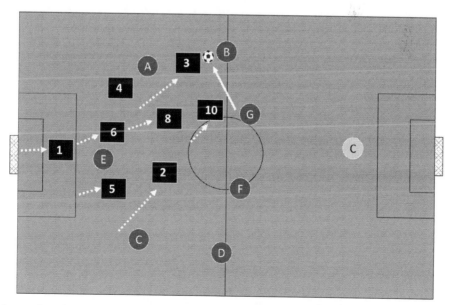

(10) forces the sideways pass and this can also result in pushing up a few yards from the back as well as pressing the ball. The coach is the target for the defending team to play to when they win the ball and is also a support player for the attacking team.

The longer the arrows the greater the distance travelled up the field each time

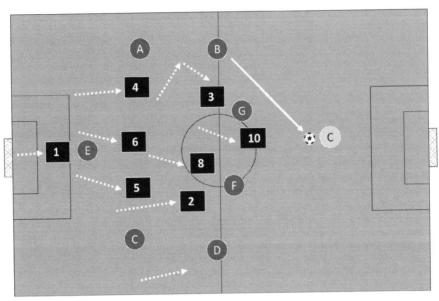

(3) presses so well that (B) has only a back pass to make. (8) and (10) are in passing lanes to stop a forward pass. (3) positions to stop a pass to (A). As the ball travels this gives the team a real chance to push up several more yards and potentially leave (E) offside.

Danger from a first time delivery from the coach to (A) or (C)

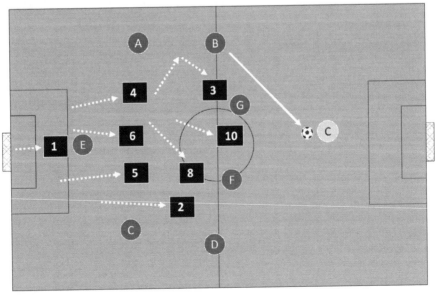

(10) does not press the coach as doing so would put himself out of position and the coach is too far away to stop a delivery. (3) moves inside to press (G), (8) moves up and across to press (F). If the coach passes to (D) then (2) can slide across quickly, as will (8) and (10).

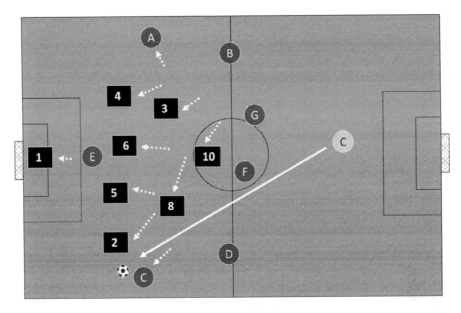

(E) is still offside but not interfering with play. (A) and (C) move wide to find more space and the coach plays to (C). The defending team now need to drop back and across and lose some ground. Midfield three condense back and across to where the ball is. Back 4 try to leave (E) offside still so don't recover all the way goal-side. But we are still in good defensive shape.

Alternatively anticipating the long ball behind them from the coach

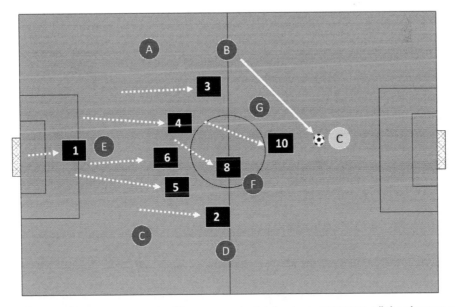

As the ball is travelling we get a great call from our central defender to PRESS UP. All the players must do so, no hesitation. Now 3 players are CLEARLY OFFSIDE. Midfield players get as tight as possible to their immediate opponents by pressing up quickly as well. (10) is not close enough to intercept the pass from the coach but is close enough to press quickly and perhaps force a mistake. Now we are almost up to the half way line and haven't touched the ball yet.

What might happen?

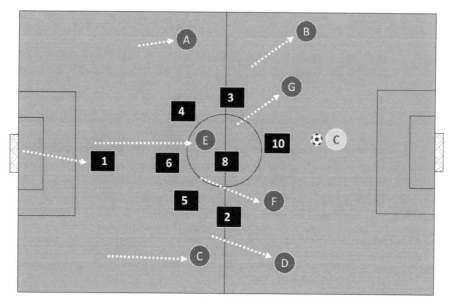

If there is no forward pass for the coach then the attacking players may need to drop off to find space to receive and build the play again. So now the START POSITION of the back four is actually almost on the half way line, not the edge of the box. (E) definitely has a long run back to be onside. Strikers HATE to have to do this; run in the wrong direction!!

Keeper - Sweeper

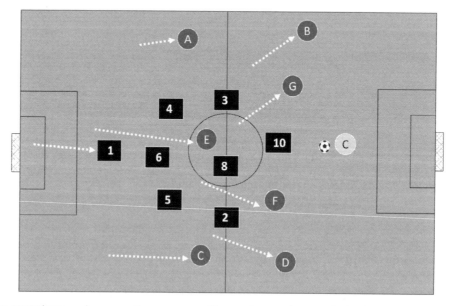

Now we MUST have our keeper as the sweeper and he must move closer to the back 3 to cover for a through ball and clean it up if they catch us out. This is just to guard against our defense getting caught flat footed with a ball in behind.

Force the error through quick pressure and we intercept the pass and win the ball

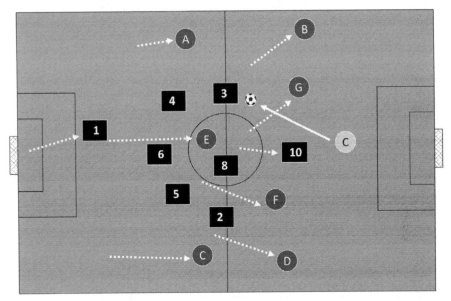

Now we MUST have our keeper as the sweeper and he must move closer to the back 3 to cover for a through ball and clean it up if they catch us out. (10) presses aggressively and forces a bad pass by the coach to (A) and (3) intercepts. You can have 2 small goals to play into to score or back into the coach, or to a big goal.

We are high but no pressure on the ball presents problems behind

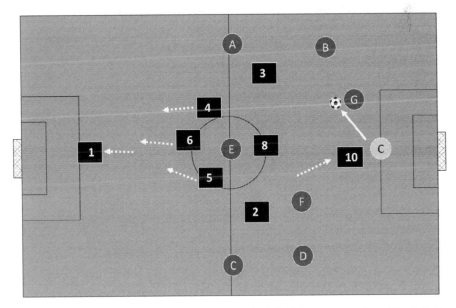

We got up to the half way line and achieved our goal but still don't have possession of the ball. Now they have a free player (G) with no pressure who likely who will play it long behind us. An immediate shout of DROP is needed to guard against this. This must be in ANTICIPATION of the forward pass. Even if it doesn't arrive we are still in command.

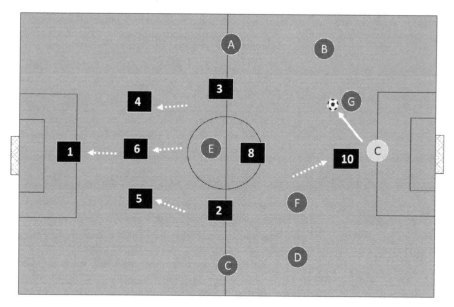

Lots of time and space to receive the long pass under no pressure and start our own build up.
This may even prevent (G) from playing the long pass and give us more time to adjust.
We are still in a strong defensive position.

Midfield players must track the runners who will be ONSIDE running from deep

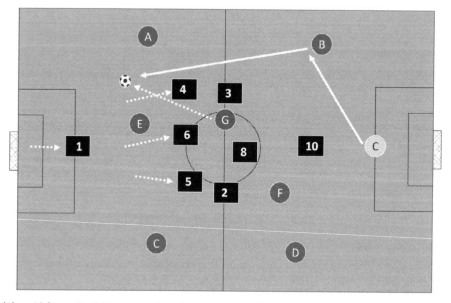

(A), (C) and (E) are all offside but not interfering with play. (G) makes a run from VERY deep and gets in behind our back THREE who have pressed up to leave 3 players offside. It's imperative our midfield players (in this case (3)), track these runners or the opponents could easily score from this movement.

Finally take out conditions and let it go free

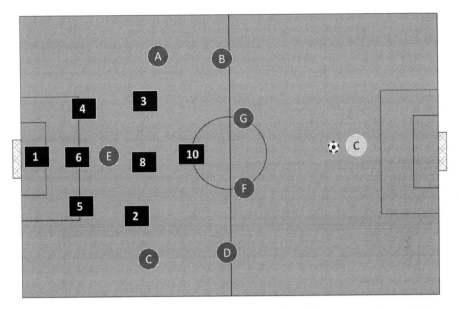

Now the big test for the defense but they can now tackle and the opponents can dribble.

Attacking Team Play in the 3-3-1-3

Distribution from the keeper and Playing out from the back

I am a real purist at heart so this would be how I want my teams to play from the back. Ok, it's risky sometimes, but to me we have to try it. We have to get away from the old fashioned "long ball from the keeper" mentality. That to me is the completely wrong way to play. When our goalkeeper has the ball, WE HAVE POSSESSION! Why kick it long and give ourselves at best a 50% chance of keeping it?

Boot it and hope you win the 2nd ball? Bad, sad and it makes me mad!!

We owe it to the players to teach them this as early as possible. So here we develop play from the back. I work on this initially practicing all ways to get out. Have opponents only intercepting passes to begin. Then let it go free.

When opponents win it back we work on the defending team condensing and defending correctly. So certain plays are recognized consciously first of all with particular CUES. If three or four ways to develop play are done frequently then it becomes a subconscious decision to move into position, so in fact no decision making is required. The reactions and movements become second nature.

Functional Exercises for Building Play from the back

Attacking shape through 4 players

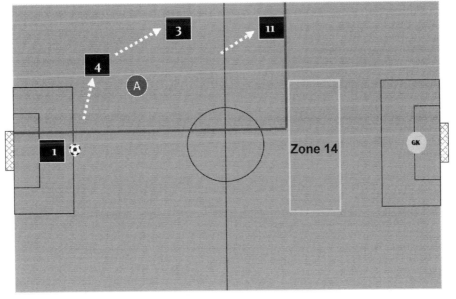

A functional practice developing movement between 3 players and the keeper. Make it easy for success initially with a 4 v 1. It is exactly the same on the other side with (2), (7) and (5) so we don't need to repeat it. You can cone off the main area you are using to show where the focus on the session is on the field.

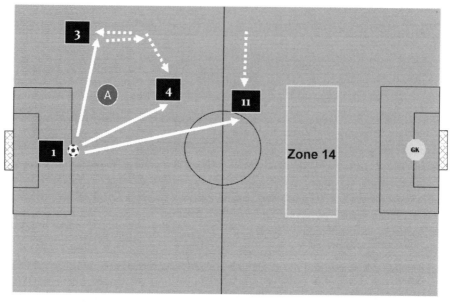

Three choices here which will depend on how the defender reacts. He could press (3) or track (4).

Inverted wing back movement

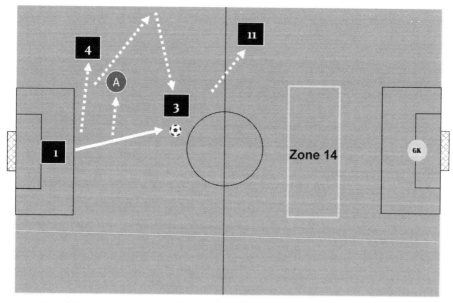

Center back (4) goes wide drawing (A) towards the touchline and (3) moves inside to receive the pass from the keeper.

Inverted wide striker move

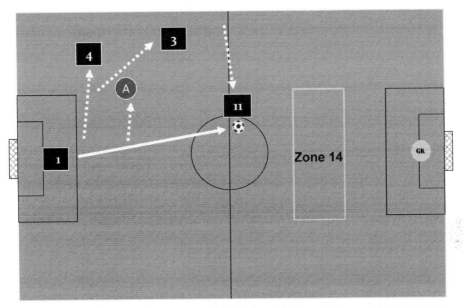

Center back (4) goes wide drawing (A) towards the touchline and (11) moves inside to receive the pass from the keeper.

Attacking shape through 5 players

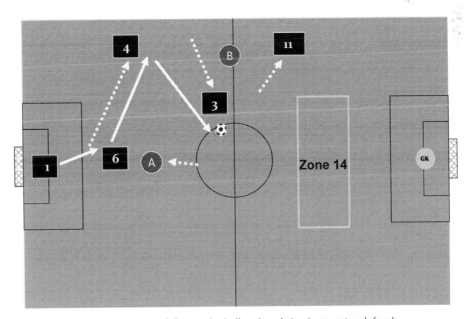

Same idea but now (6) is on the ball and we bring in an extra defender.
Inverted wing back run into space to get free from the defender.

Defender tracks the run inside

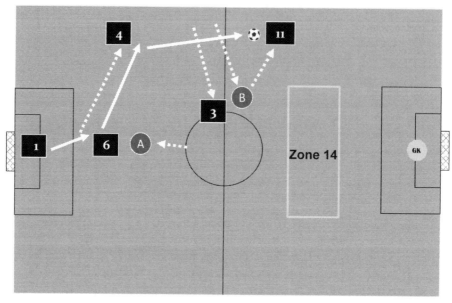

The inverted wing back run inside into the space to receive. Defender tracks the run so it opens up the passing lane to (11).

Three movements create space for (11)

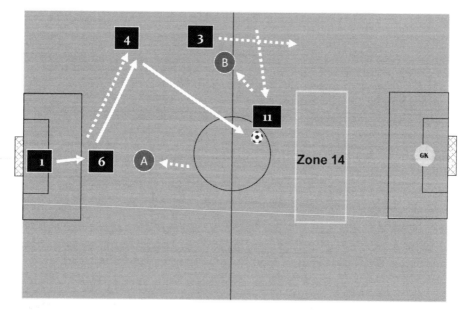

Defender (A) cuts off the pass inside so (6) passes to (4). Defender (B) presses (3) and (11) cuts inside with the inverted run to receive from center back (4). Wing Back (3) can continue an attacking forward run into the space vacated by (11).

Getting free through the center back (4)

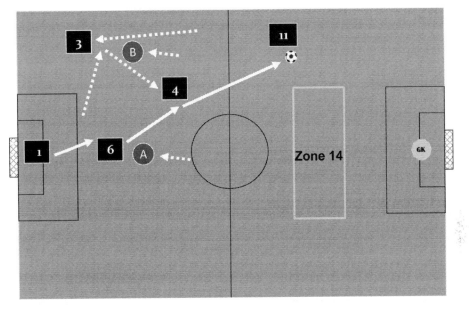

An Inverted center back (4) run to get free to receive the ball. Initial run is wide to offer support. But defender (B) closes down (4). Wing back (3) distracts (B) with a run to allow center back (4) to cut inside to get out.

Now against 3 defenders

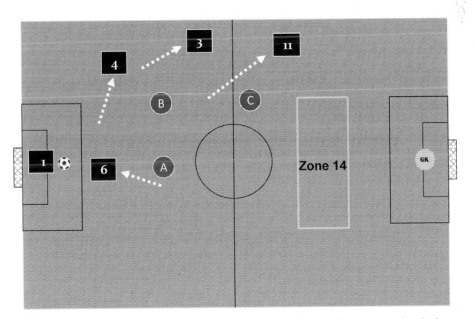

This is our offensive set up. 3 players in wide areas along the touchline. We have a 4 v 3 plus the keeper so it will be much harder work to get free from the back. Have defenders not press immediately to get the session going, more shadowing the player but they can intercept passes.

Now looking for imaginative solutions to build from the back

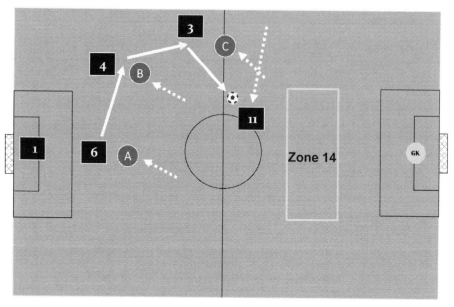

Ask defenders to make decisions to press a player. This will mean one player should be free somewhere. In this case it is (11).

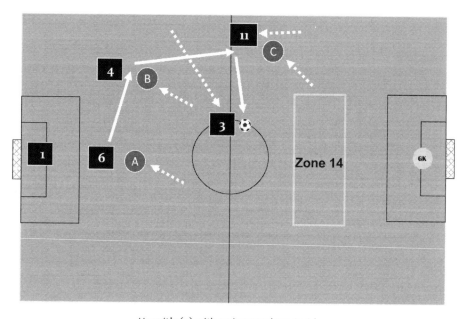

Here it's (3) with an inverted run inside.

Rotation of (11) and (3)

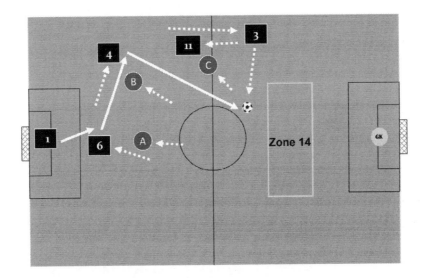

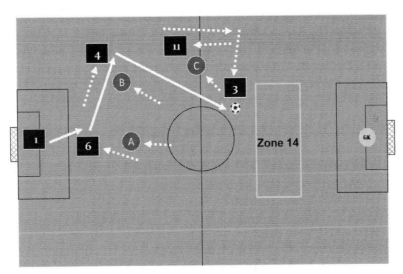

Defender (C) closes down (11) after (3) and (11) interchange and (3) makes a second run inside to receive the pass into space.

There are different ways to motivate the attacking team building from the back to get an end product. They can get a goal by building and then passing to the coach to restart, actually score in the big goals, have two small goals for them to score in, or as I have previously stated, have them KEEP the ball, working it up and back and across until they lose it.

The defending team, if they win it, can attack THE GOAL TO TRY TO SCORE. You can keep count of the score to keep it competitive. Increase the number of attacking players as the defending team get better at building from the back to increase the difficulty.

Distribution from the keeper and Playing from the back

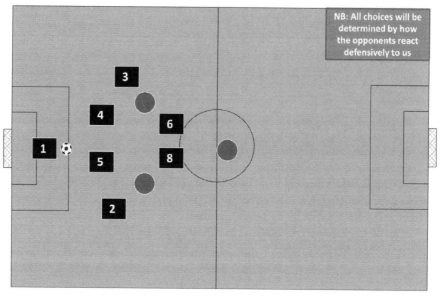

Perhaps use cones instead of actual players to practice to make it work initially and to gain confidence (better still use Mannequins).

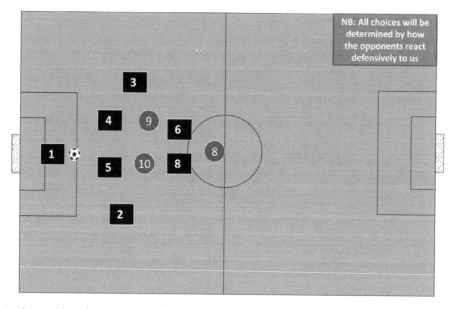

Our starting position, the team is in defensive shape and ready to attack. A 6 v 3 makes it easy to get out, but decrease the number of opponents if necessary to gain success initially.

1. Distribution from the keeper using one attacking wing fullback

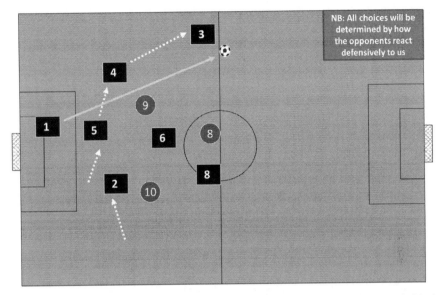

We attack down one side and slide across with the back three to cover the spaces behind.

2. Distribution through both center backs or (6)

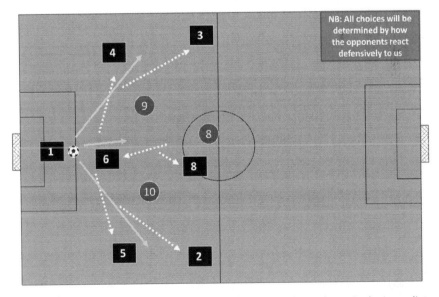

A simple starting position on distribution from the back using only those players in the immediate vicinity.
A 3 v 2 at the back in our favor.

3. Distribution through Number (6) in a wide area

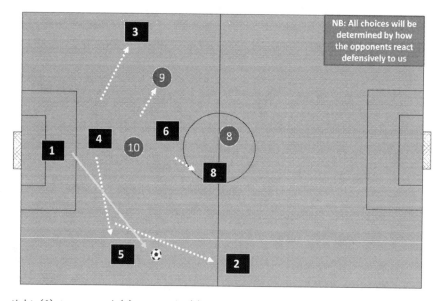

Now (6) breaks wide to receive the ball and escape being marked in the middle. The same can happen with (6) breaking out to the right also, replacing (5) who stays central.

4. Distribution from the keeper: One centre back breaks wide

(4) stays tight, (6) stays central, (5) goes wide, (2) pushes on and we get out down one side. Opponents (H) and (L) stop our (6) and (4), (5) gets free to play out. Only 2 defending now, so risky against a counter attack.

5. Distribution from the keeper thru wingbacks

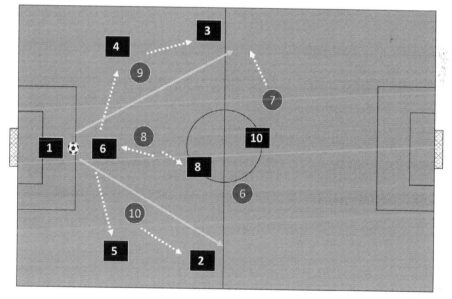

If they push 3 up, we can get out through our wingbacks. Have opponents make different choices to force the keeper to make relevant decisions in training.

We can start to add players and build the session up. Here we close off one side so the keeper has to recognize he cant go to (3) but can go to (2).

6. Distribution from the keeper thru INVERTED wingbacks

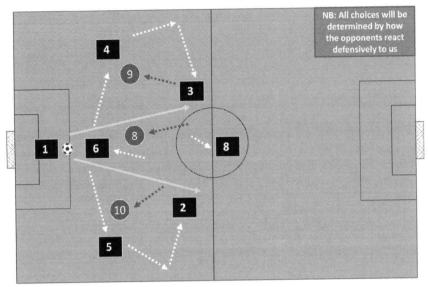

Wing fullbacks (2) and (3) cut inside to receive the ball.

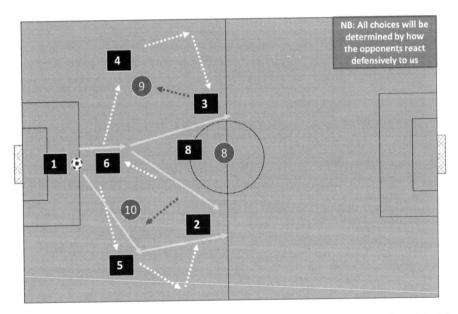

Wing fullbacks (2) and (3) cut inside to receive the ball and can receive the pass from (4), (5) or (6) also in the buildup.

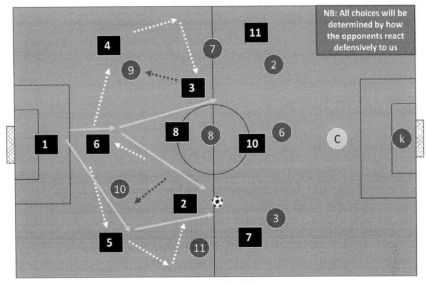

Wing fullbacks (2) and (3) cut inside to receive the ball and can receive the pass from (4) , (5) or (6) also in the buildup.

7. Distribution from the keeper thru central midfield rotation of (6) and (8)

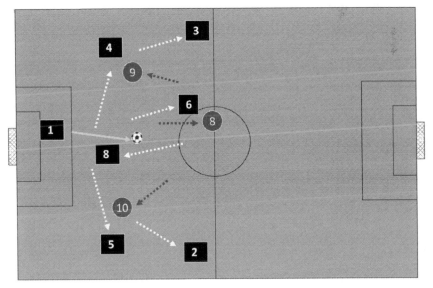

(6) clears the space and takes the opponent (8) with him and our (8) drops in free to start the attack. Can also be with (6) and (10).

8. Distribution through Both wing backs dropping back

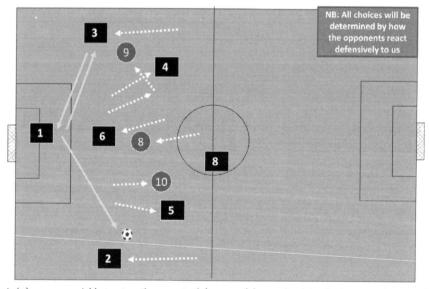

Centre backs both push out quickly and they are tracked by the two strikers. This releases spaces behind them. Both wing backs drop back into those spaces to receive the ball.

9. Switching the play back through the keeper to the other side

Their (9) presses quickly to stop the pass to (4) so our (3) goes back to the keeper who switches the play to our (2) on the other side.

10. Distribution through Center backs pushing out

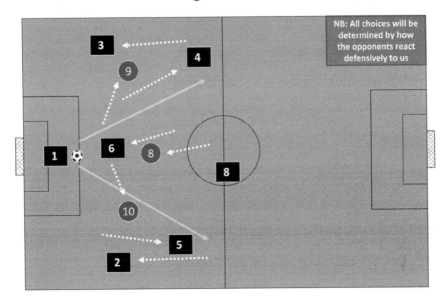

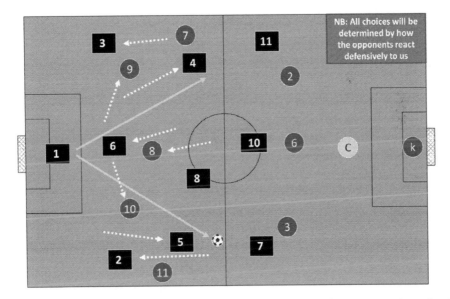

Wing full backs drop back in. They are tracked by the two strikers. This releases spaces down the sides.
Both wing backs drop back into those spaces to open it up for the center backs.

11. Distribution from the back through inverted wingers

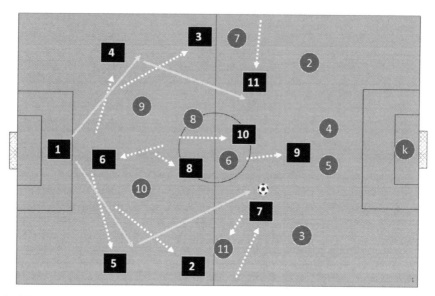

Here we build play and spread out 3 players on each touchline. At the right moment winger / wide striker (7) cuts inside to attack the inside space. Their (11) gets drawn to our (2).

Distribution from the keeper and Playing from the back 11 v 11

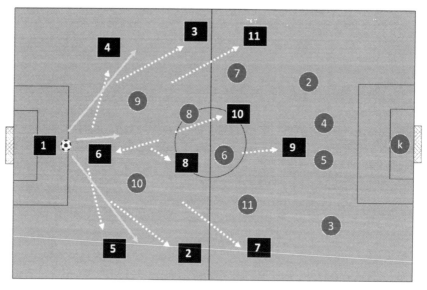

Now in an 11 v 11. Our normal way to get out from the back. We should always try this initially if it is on to do so. Try to get out thru (4), (5) or (6).

Distribution from the keeper 11 v 11

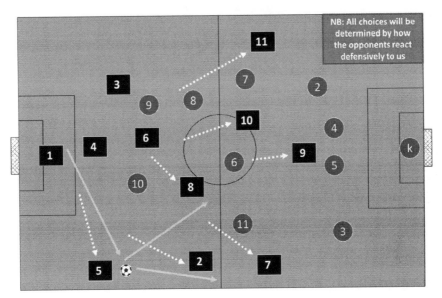

Another way to get out thru one center back and one wingback and even (8).

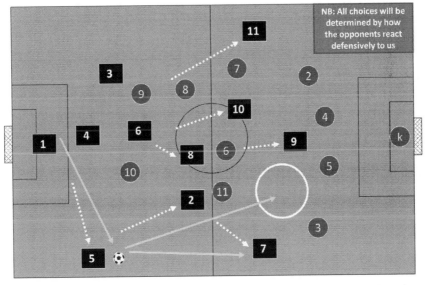

Another way to get out through one center back (5) and (7). Wingback (2) tucks inside and may take opponent (11) with them to clear the pass for (7). The circled area is also a nice area to play into.

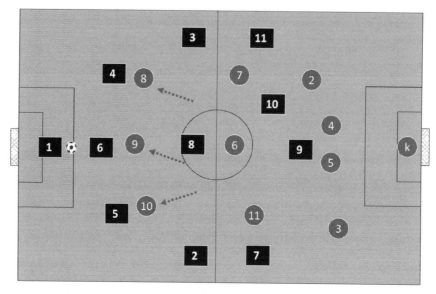

They go 3 v 3 against us to stop us playing out of the back so we try to get out through (2) and (3). Otherwise we have to push up, condense and kick it long.

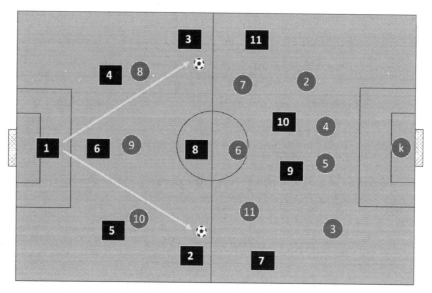

They go 3 v 3 against us so we try to get out through (2) and (3). Otherwise we have to push up, condense and kick it long. They "may" see what we are doing and push 7 and 11 onto our wingbacks (2) and (3).

They push two players onto our wingbacks (2) and (3)

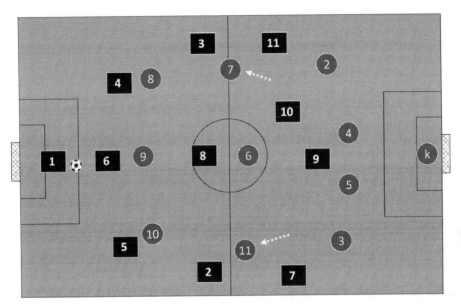

This outlet is now stopped, so we have to change our team shape from "wide and long" to "short and tight", getting ready for the long kick from the keeper.

12. They have pushed onto our Wingbacks so this outlet is stopped. We have to go long as a last resort

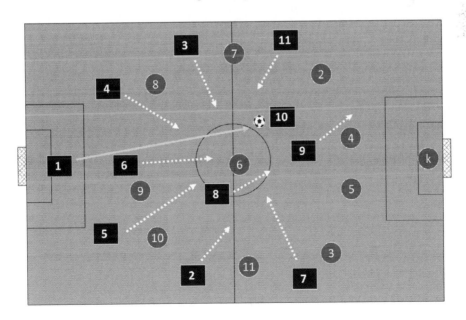

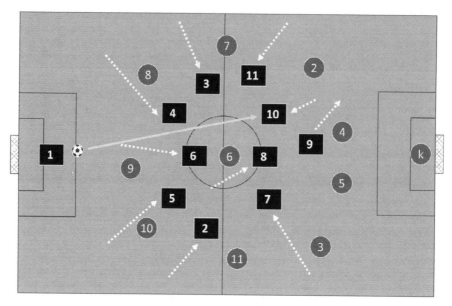

This can still be EFFECTIVE: Now we condense as a team "short and tight". Our (10) is good in the air so we hit him and we have a lot of players around him to win the 2nd ball. Of course opponents will readjust also. It's cat and mouse.

We leave their 3 strikers offside.

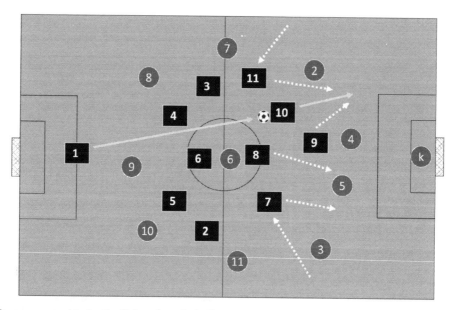

Players can gamble for the flick on from (10). Players position behind, in front and alongside (10) so wherever the 2nd ball goes we have players to pick it up. WE ABSOLUTELY MUST get better at this. Obviously, opponents will position better than this defensively; but you get the point.

Spatial Awareness and Movement OFF the Ball

Positioning correctly "off the ball" is vital for team success

Positioning between opponents using CONES for reference

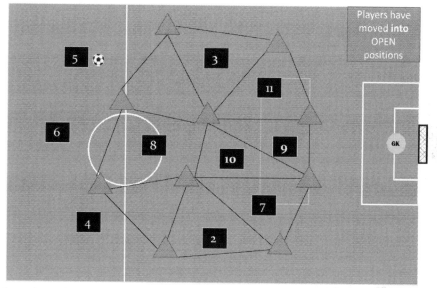

This is how players have moved to find space using cone positions to help them, finding the best space between triangles and diamond shapes of cones. This is also determined by the position of the ball.

Poor positioning between opponents

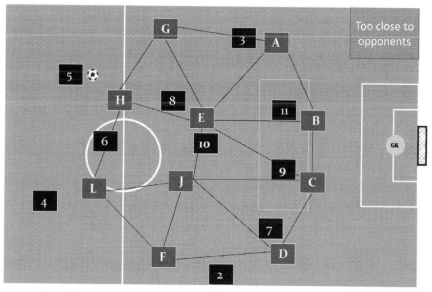

A few examples of how being out of position by just a few yards makes it harder for (5) to pass the ball and for the receiver to receive it. Not using SPACE correctly can be costly.

Poor positioning due to opponents closing down

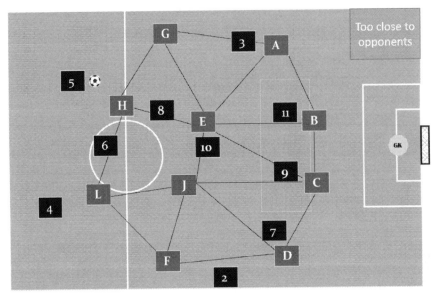

Players are constantly moving to either find SPACE or mark an opponent. These current positions may be at the actual moment a player is closed down. This is when our players need to MOVE AGAIN.

As a start position between opponents

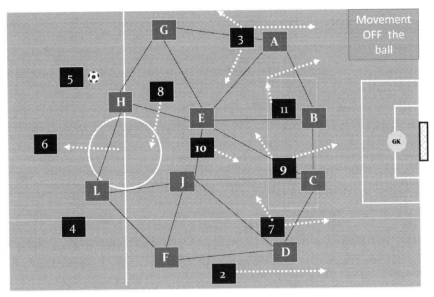

As long as the players don't stay in these positions but MOVE, potentially as shown, then we can make it work. These are just suggestions of movement that are more obvious given the set up.

Positioning between opponents

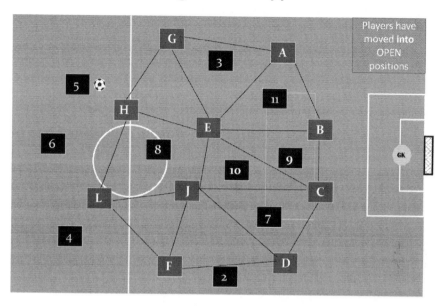

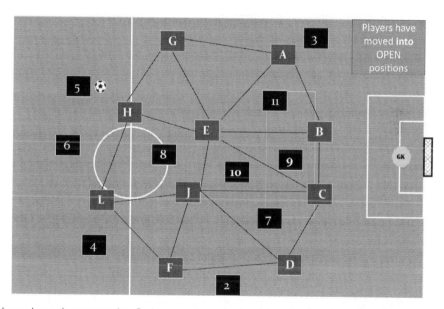

This is how players have moved to find space using opponents' positions to help them. They try to find the best space between triangles and diamond shapes of opponents. This is also determined by the position of the ball.

Positioning between each other

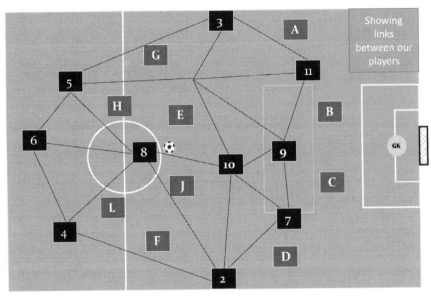

Now challenging players to make decisions. Does (B) or (C) close down (9), for example? Does (D) or (C) close down (11)?

How movement of a player can help another player

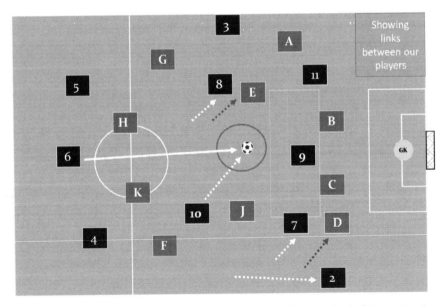

A simple movement by (8) takes defender (E) away and clears the space for (10) to receive the pass. Likewise, (7) takes defender (D) inside and clears the space for wingback (2).

A FOUR player Rotation

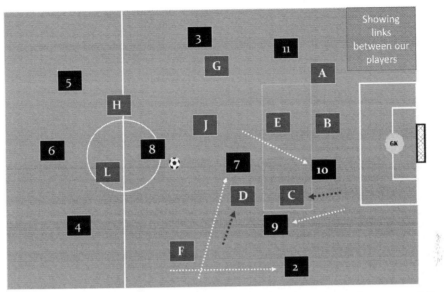

Movements affect the positioning of defenders and FREE up spaces for our players potentially.
Pass to (2) and (10) in front; (9) to feet; (7) into his path.

A FOUR player Rotation shown without all opponents

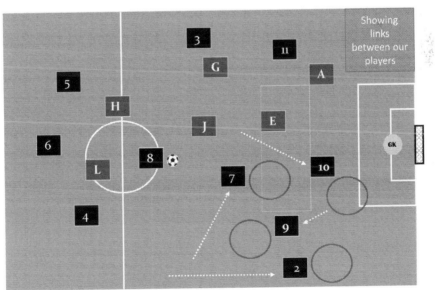

Perhaps more clarity now; FREEING up spaces for our players potentially. Pass to (2) and (10) in front,
(9) to feet and (7) into his path.

Simple 2 player Rotational Combination Movements

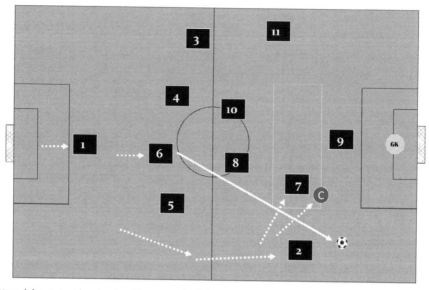

Now (7) cuts inside, clearing the space for (2) to overlap. (6) plays the ball into the space (7) has created for (2).

How to Develop Rotational Awareness in a 3-3-1-3
From very simple 2 player rotations to more complex 6 player rotations

Simple 2 player Rotational Combination Movements

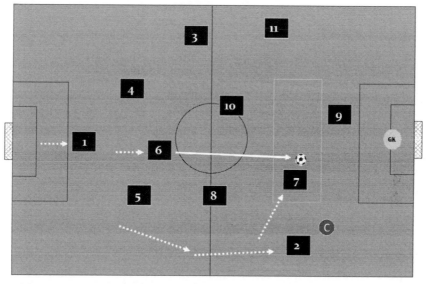

Now (7) cuts inside clearing the space for (2) to overlap. Defender (C) stays wide to mark (2) so (6) passes to (7).

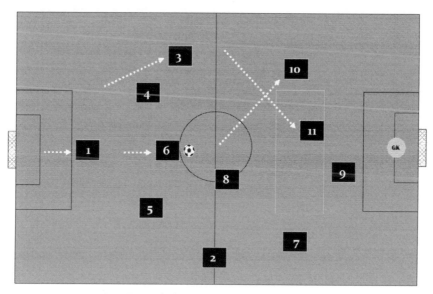

Now central midfielder (10) and wide left striker / midfielder (11) rotate.

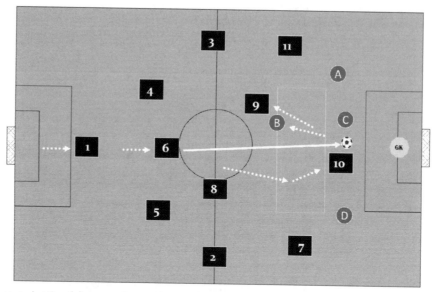

Now central striker (9) comes short and central midfielder (10) goes long and (6) plays the ball to (10) into the space created by (9) by bringing defender (B) out of it.

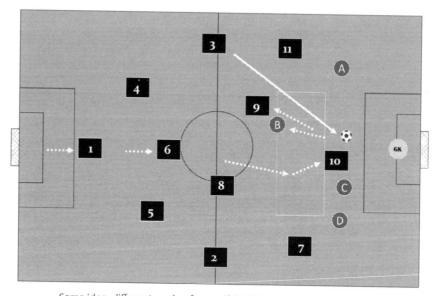

Same idea, different angle of pass. This REALLY is a simple rotation.

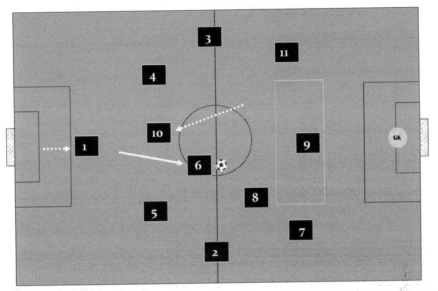

Now center back (6) brings the ball out of defense and central midfielder (10) drops in to cover. Fullbacks (2) or (3) could also drop in to cover (6).

Simple 3 player Rotational Combination Movements

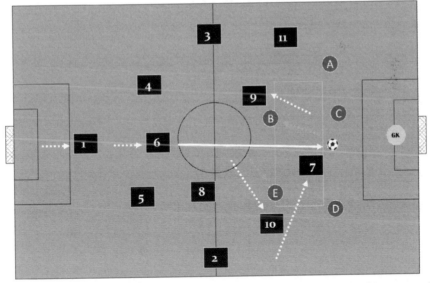

(9) short, (10) wide, (7) inside from out. So (9) becomes (10), (10) becomes (7), (7) becomes (9).

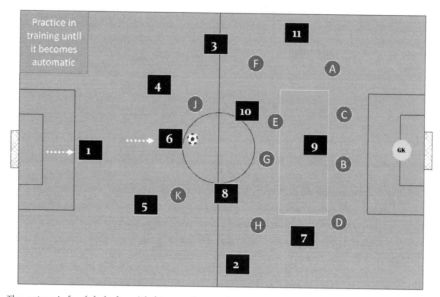

The set up is for (3), (10) and (11) to work together and move opponents around to free up space for each other

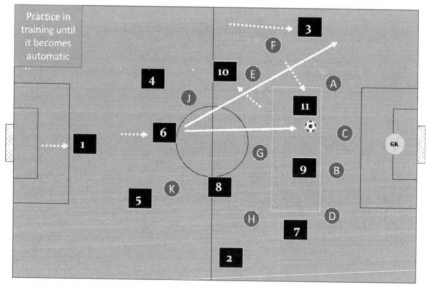

We hope the defenders react slowly to our movements so they are not aware of what we are going to do which should give us the edge. (9) can pull away to clear the space for (11) also.

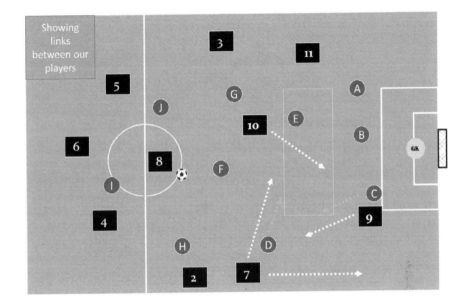

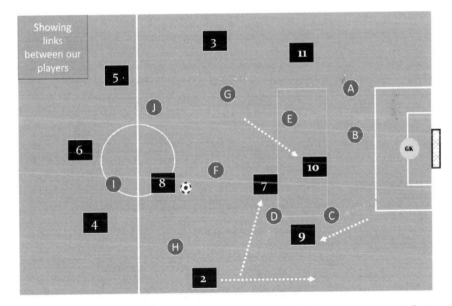

Movements affect the positioning of defenders and FREE up spaces for our players potentially. Here are the "start positions" of the attacking players. Pass to (2) and (10) in front, (9) to feet and (7) into his path.

Simple 4 player Rotational Combination Movements

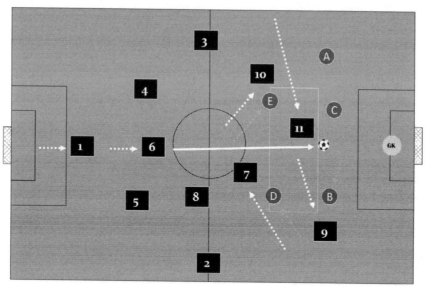

(9) wide, (10) wide, (11) inside from outside. So, (10) becomes (11), (11) becomes (9) and (9) becomes (7) and (7) becomes (10).

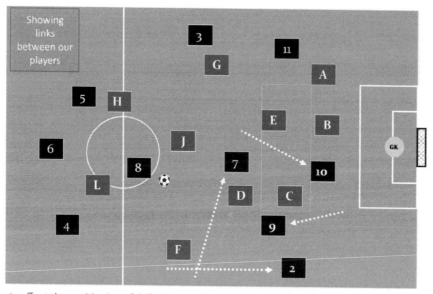

Movements affect the positioning of defenders and FREE up spaces for our players potentially. Here are the "start positions" of the attacking players. Pass to (2) and (10) in front, (9) to feet and (7) into his path.

A FOUR player Rotation shown without opponents

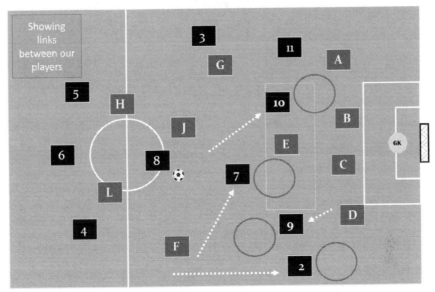

Perhaps more clarity now; FREEING up spaces for our players potentially.
Pass to (2) and (10) in front, (9) to feet and (7) into his path.

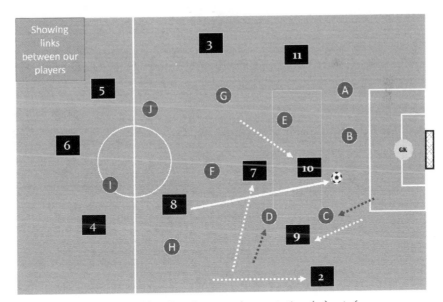

Now include (2) and we have a 4 player rotation. (10) gets free.

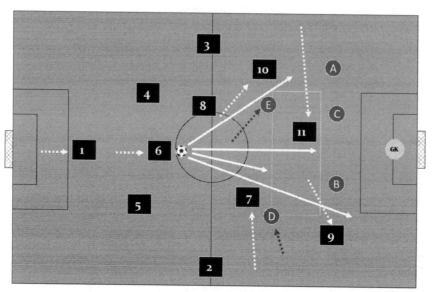

(9) wide, (10) wide, (11) inside from outside. Movements create space for each other and for themselves. So, (10) becomes (11), (11) becomes (9) and (9) becomes (7) and (7) becomes (8). (9) moves off the shoulder of (B).

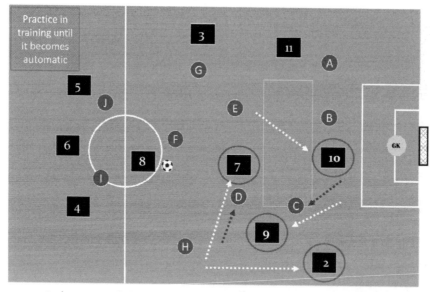

Perhaps more clarity now; FREEING up spaces for our players potentially. Pass to (2) and (10) in front, (9) to feet and (7) into his path.

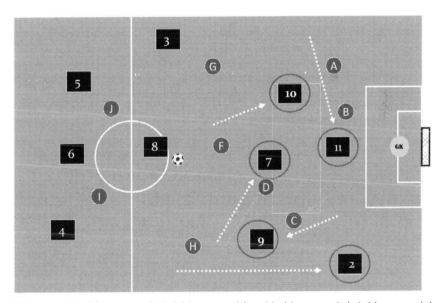

Here we get (2) free in an inside right position between (C) and (D). (7) distracts (D)

A FIVE player Rotation shown with opponents

(2) becomes (7), (7) becomes (10); (9) becomes (7) and (10) becomes (11), (11) becomes (9).

A SIX player rotation shown with opponents

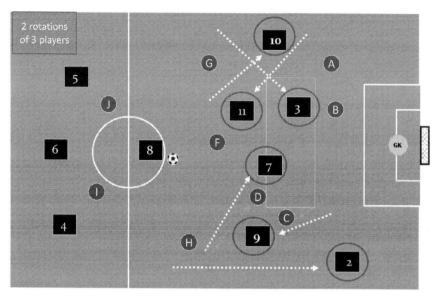

(2) becomes (7), (7) becomes (10); (9) becomes (7) and (10) becomes (11), (3) becomes (9).
(11) becomes an inside left player in no mans land. We want ALL players to appear in "off" and
unpredictable positions on the field like this.

How movement of a player can help another player

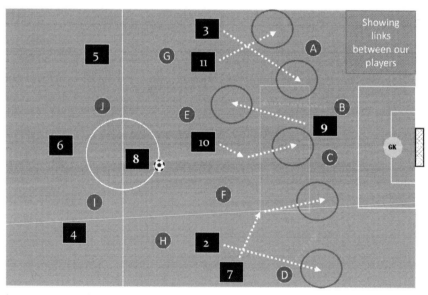

A 6 player rotation with 3 separate rotations of 2 players each. Here we show the start positions of
each player and where we want them to end up.

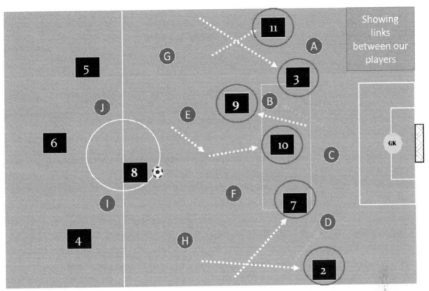

A 6 player rotation with 3 separate rotations of 2 players each. This is the picture after all the movement has happened. Hopefully we will get a few players FREE out of the 6 players interchanging.

Forward movement and rotations to create options for the player on the ball to pass behind the defense

This section addresses those times when the ball needs to be played in behind a defense holding a high line. Players learn forward movement and the timing and angle of runs and creating several options for the passer.

They defend high, we play in behind

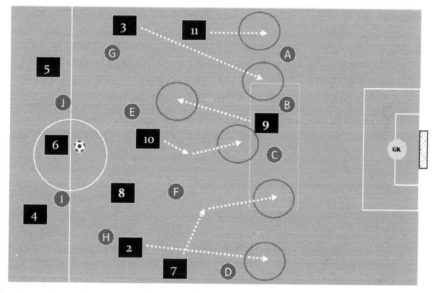

A 6 player rotation with 3 separate rotations of 2 players each. Here we show the start positions of the players and where we want them to end up.

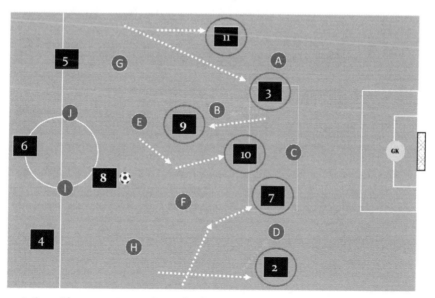

A 6 player rotation with 3 separate rotations of 2 players each. This is after all the movement has happened. Hopefully, we will get a few players FREE out of the 6 players interchanging.

A very offensive attack

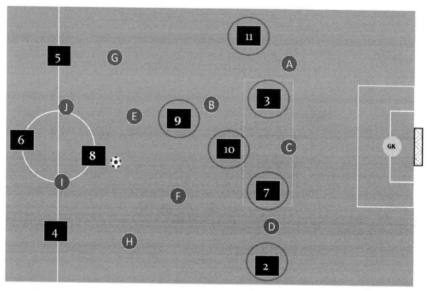

Many passing opportunities now for (6) after players interchange to move defenders into places they don't want to go.

The set up to promote angled support

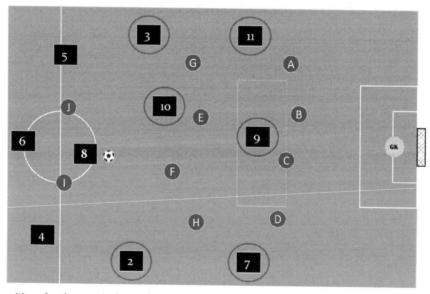

Start positions for the attack players forming big spaces between each other to open up passing lanes. We get as BIG as possible.

(9) is the catalyst to the attack

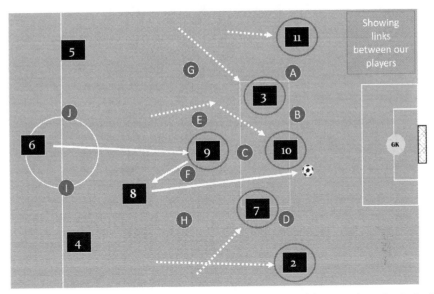

(9) holds the ball up to lay off for a third man run by (10). As soon as (9) comes short that is the "cue" for the others to attack forward. Timing is the key.

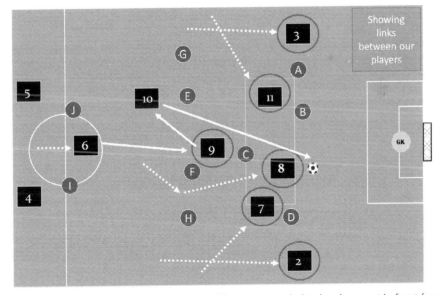

(9) holds the ball up to lay off for a third man run by (8). So support behind and support in front for the next pass. It could go to any of the attacking players so we have several third man runs.

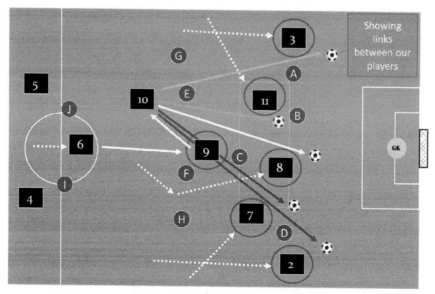

Showing all the potential passes for (10) on the ball. With all the rotations / interchanges and movements OFF the ball; someone will get free, (9) has to pick them out.

Switching the Point of Attack

Here we show how to overload one side of the field to leave the other side open to catch opponents with a fast switching of play. Rather than player rotation, this is BALL rotation and retention.

Attacking set up

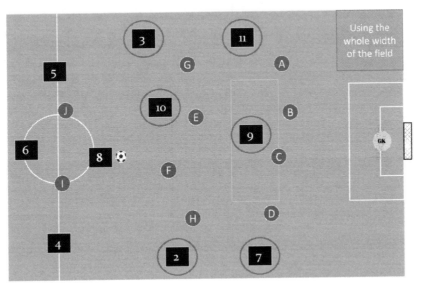

Start positions for the attack players forming big spaces between each other to open up passing lanes. We get as BIG as possible. We will next begin to overload one side of the field and make it the strong side.

Drawing defenders towards the ball

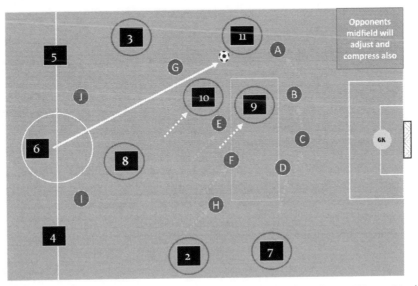

We play (11) in wide but keep players on the weak side of the field wide and open. We want to draw the opponents towards the ball with our initial movements of players close to the ball and drawing them away from the WEAK side. Here you see (2) and (7) almost forgotten and on the BLIND / WEAK SIDE of play.

Switching the point of attack through 3 passes

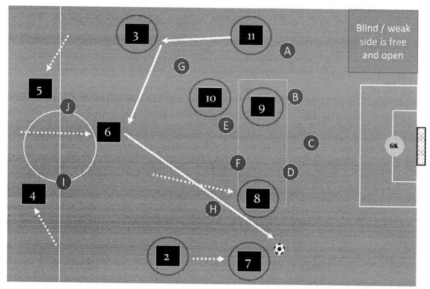

(6) releases himself from the back and now we play two very fast passes to change the point of attack. (8) gets involved also on the blind / weak side of the field, catching the opponents off guard.

Being patient to create the switch

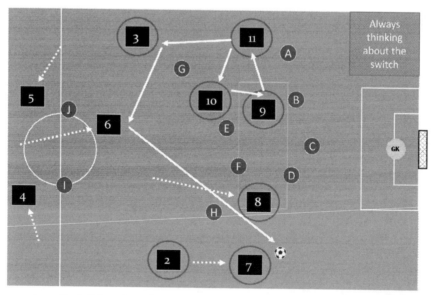

We may even keep the ball there for a few passes to draw them in even more, being patient and showing no interest for the other side of the field. Then we hit them hard with the fast switch of play and we have 3 players in wide open space to attack the goal.

Not showing defenders' obvious recovery runs for clarity

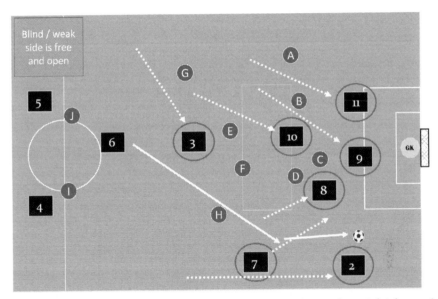

Now (2) overlaps (7) to get into a crossing position and in the meantime as the switch is happening (8), (9), (10) and (11) get in finishing positions in and around the box. (6) is ready to drop back in should the opponents win the ball and counter attack

Developing Play in the Attacking Third

Do this as a shadow play at first for success, then bring passive defenders in, then play real with defenders defending correctly.

The start position is the ball into the feet of Striker (9)

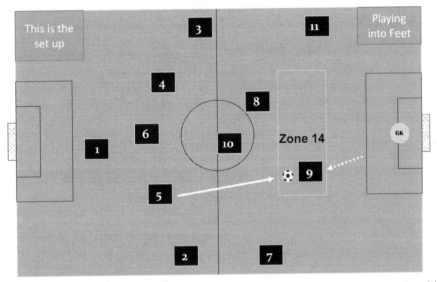

This can be from a free kick or in open play. We work a "set play" in open play where, when (5) is on the ball, (2), (7), (9) and (10) and others already know what to do BEFORE the ball is delivered.

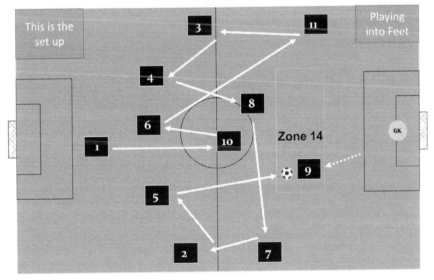

Have the team pass around and develop the play, then at some point play to (4) or (5). That is the CUE to pass to (9) dropping off short to start the movement.

Potential Options

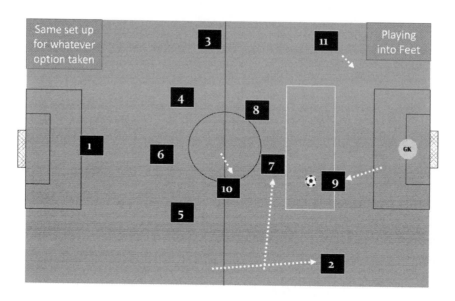

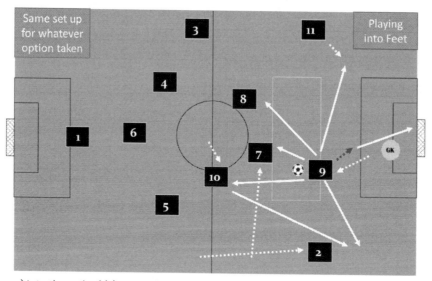

Options: a) Into the path of (7) to attack on goal or shoot; b) lay off to (10) to pass to (2) or switch play to (8) or (11), c) (9) lays off directly to (2) to cross, d) (9) spins and plays the other way to (11); e) (9) can receive and turn and shoot if open.

Start position is the ball into the feet of Striker (9)

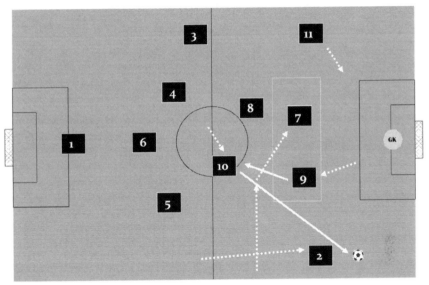

Timing is important now. (7) runs inside, clearing the space for (2) to run into, (9) lays the ball off, (10) plays it into (2)'s path. We work to get into the box.

Movements off the ball into and around the box

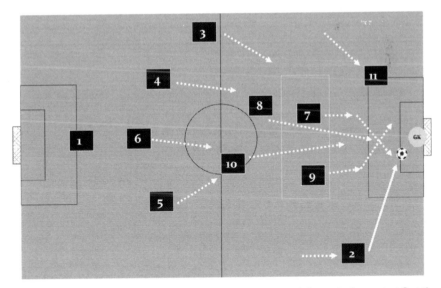

(7) attacks far post first then switches to attack the near post. (9) attacks far post at first then switches to attack the near post. (8) positions behind (7) and (9) centrally for the pull back, (10) positions on the edge of the box, (11) for anything hit too long from (2).

In and Around the box final positioning

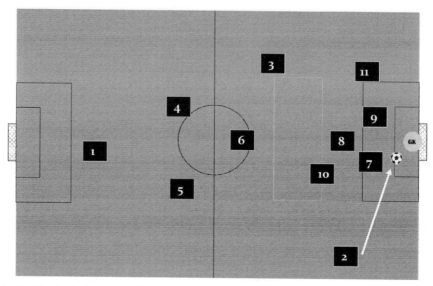

The End Product with players in pertinent positions for wherever the ball could be delivered.
Players would be closer to goal than this, which will will be shown next.

Attacking movements to get in and around the box for the cross

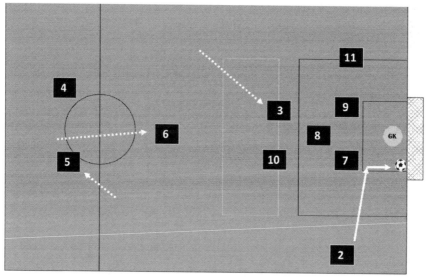

End Product, attacking 4 areas; the near post, the far post and in behind and beyond.
(10) is in position to clear the second ball and (3) may also shadow around the box.

Crossing into or around the 2nd 6 yard box

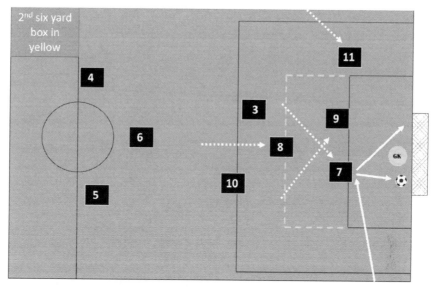

(2), who is out of the picture, delivers the cross. Players are arriving as LATE as possible and as FAST as possible. Four options for (2) and two players shadowing the box.

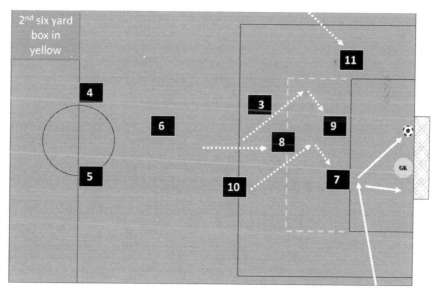

(2), who is out of the picture, delivers the cross. (7) and (9) dont necessarily need to cross-over, they can both take defenders AWAY from the crossing area and then cut back.

Players are in too early or the crosser can't play in first time

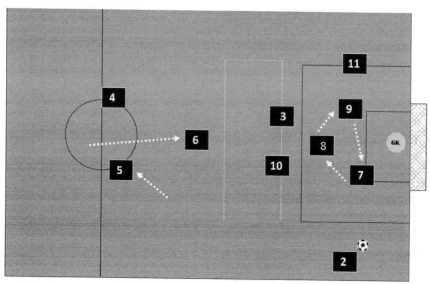

Players are in the box waiting for the cross. If the ball doesn't come first time and they stand still waiting, they are easily marked. The players may be in too early or maybe the crosser cannot get the ball in first time.

Rotation begins

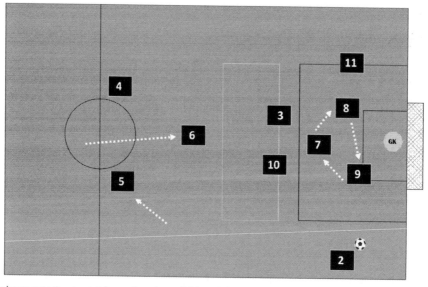

Three player rotation to get free of markers. (2) has delayed so he cannot play it in first time, therefore the 3 players are static and in too early. So (7), (9) and (8) rotate positions rather than stand still in the box and be easily marked.

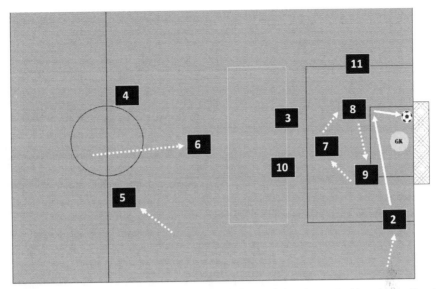

If the space is free in front of (2), he can run the ball in and give the 3 attacking players time to re-position for a ball played in on the ground with pace.

Three player rotation on the edge of the 2nd 6 yard box

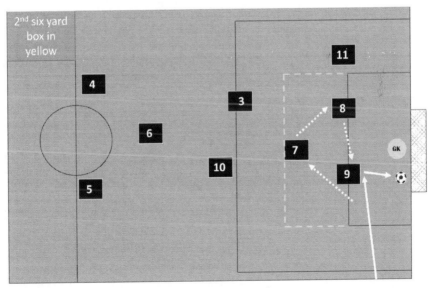

(2), out of picture, delivers the cross. The three players have rotated positions trying to free up space for each other. The other players are in ideal positions for attacking, second ball clearance and defending the counter attack.

Near post player (7) clearing the SPACE for the far post player (9)

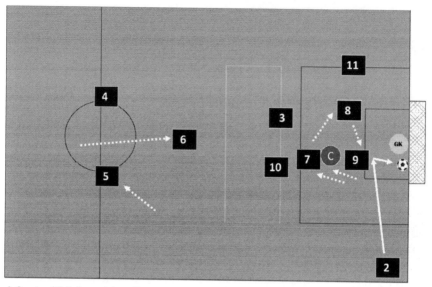

Here defender (C) follows (7) and leaves the near post space open for (9) to attack. This is what we are trying to achieve with the 3 player rotation, as someone somewhere may get free. (2) has to pick out the best option or just drive it into the box.

Near post player getting FREE for a shot on goal

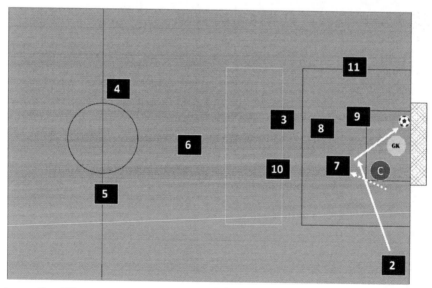

(7) drops off to (8)'s position. This means if the marker does not go with him then (2) may pull the ball back for him. Here defender (C) marks the SPACE in front of the goal instead allowing (7) room to shoot. (9) and (8) may still change positions.

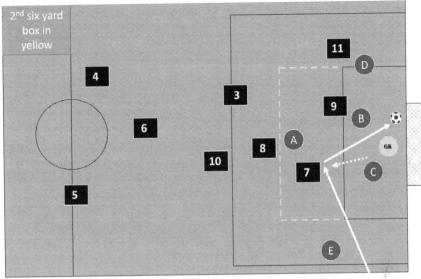

(2), out of the picture, delivers the cross. In closer detail here: (7) getting free dropping off into space in the 2nd six yard box to get a one touch shot on goal.

Clearing the near post SPACE for the far post player (9)

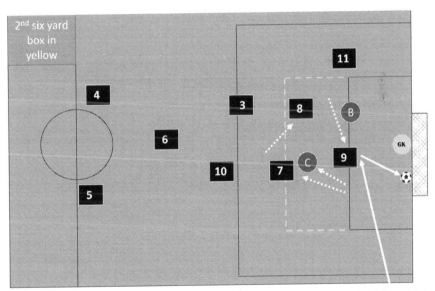

Leaving out most other defenders to make it clearer how (7), taking defender (C) out of the near post SPACE, releases (9) making the run from the far post. You hope players man mark for this particular move. (9) gets a run on defender (B).

The 3 Team Transition Game for attacking players in and around the box

1. Three teams. the outside team works with the inside attacking team. Teaches both defending and attacking play.
2. First team to score 2 goals stays on; the losing team goes off
3. Keep the score for number of wins per team
4. Transition game: If the defending team wins the ball, they must pass to the outside team to then attack.
5. Teaches the mentality of transitional change.
6. Developing Quick Play in and around the box
7. As soon as the team lose possession they must try to defend on the offside line and beyond, thus immediately pushing opponents away from the goal.
8. Using the set up through the "numbers" to suit how we set our teams up

Three team game: The Set Up

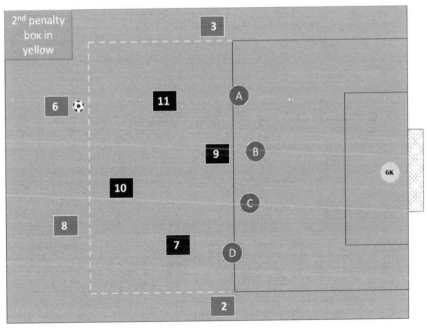

Constant transitioning from attacking to defending as possession changes

Attacking Play

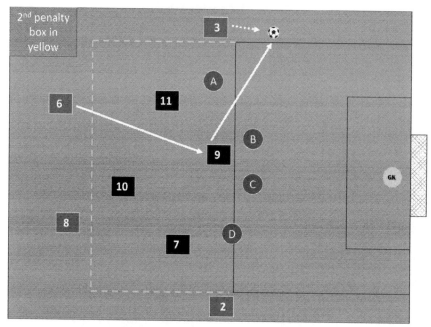

Quick break using the overlapping wingback (3).

Crossing behind the defense

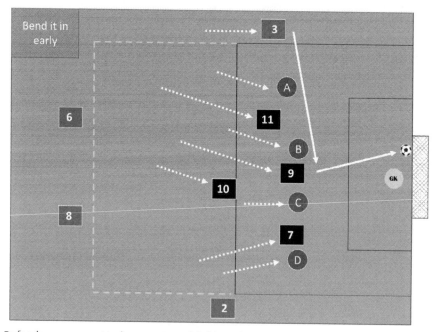

Defenders recover, attackers pressure, (3) drives the ball behind the recovering defenders.

Striker (9) moves AWAY from the ball: The Crespo

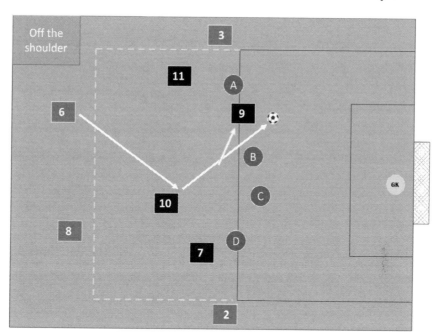

(9) off the shoulder of (B) to receive facing forward. Short and sharp movements.

Check away and back across: The Crespo

(9) off the shoulder of (B) who follows the run. (9) checks back into the space he created.

Subtle movements by the striker to get free

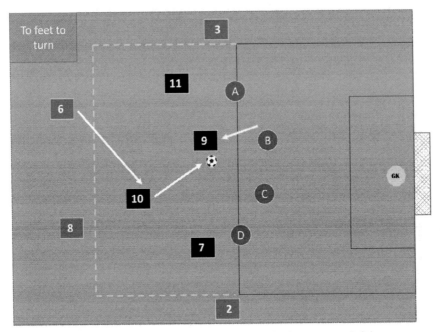

(9) checks back into space to receive to feet and side on to attack (B) 1 v 1.

Opposite Run by (9): The Vialli Check

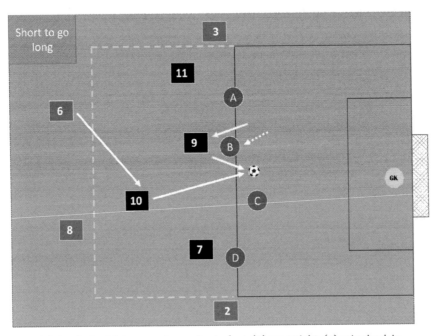

(9) checks back into space to receive to feet. (B) stays tight, (9) spins back in.

Opposite Run by (9): Del Piero Spin Away

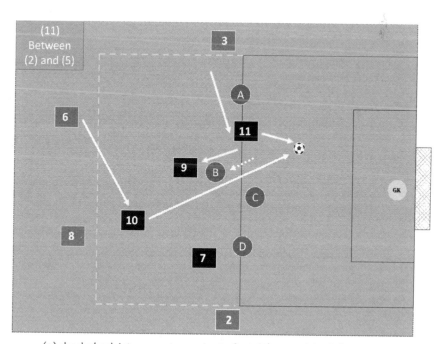

(9) checks back into space to receive to feet. (B) stays tight, (9) spins away and back in.

Short to create space behind for another player

(9) checks back into space to receive to feet. (B) stays tight, (11) cuts inside.

Check to and back: The Vialli Check

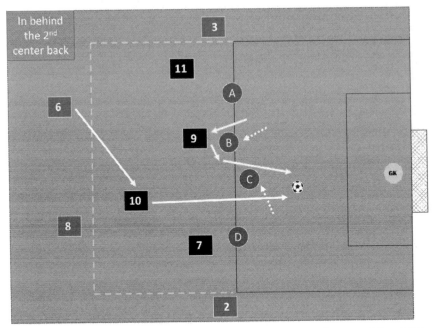

(C) tucks in to close the space as (B) gets tight. (9) reads the pass between (C) and (D).

Combination and Link Play

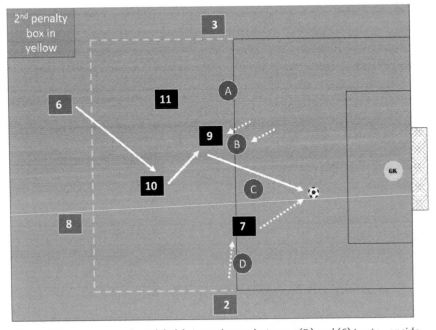

Round the corner pass from (9). (7) times the run between (D) and (C) to stay onside.

1 v 1's in and around the penalty box

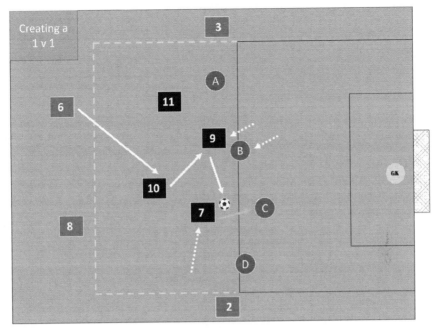

Try to create 1 v1 s for players to run at and commit opponents

Or creating give and go's: short and sharp

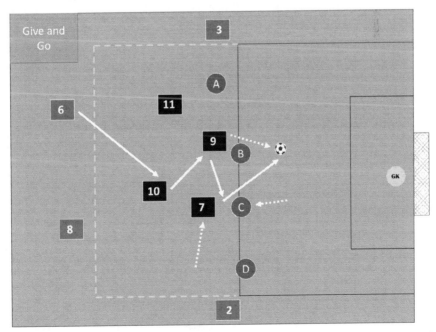

The old 1- 2 is one of the best (and simplest) moves ever. Timing of the pass and run is vital.

An Example: Creating THIRD MAN runs

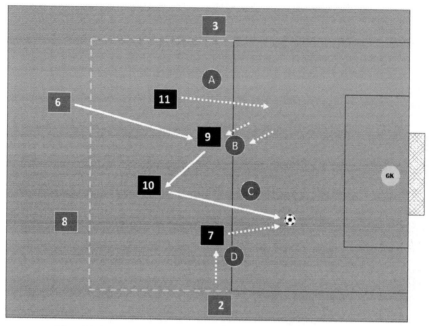

(7) and (11) provide two options in behind the opponent's back four.

Creating THIRD MAN runs: another idea

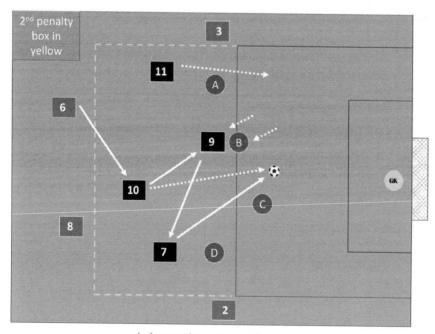

(10) starts the move and finishes it.

Blindside THIRD MAN runs

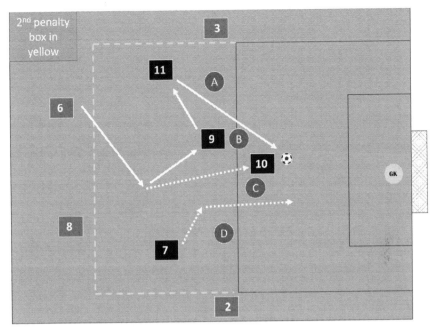

Players watch the ball go to (11) and maybe don't see the run by (10) or (7)?

Keeper saves the ball and distributes quickly

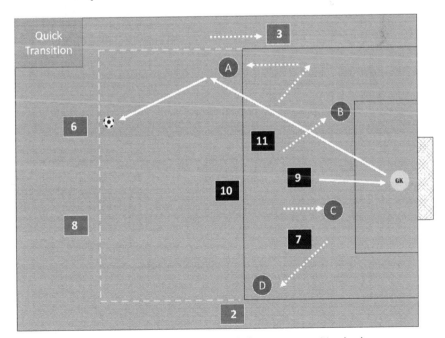

Defenders now have the ball and play out to transition back.

Now defenders are attackers

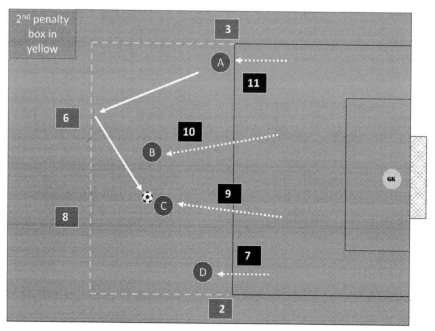

Defenders now have the ball and play out to transition back.

Defenders win the ball and now Transition

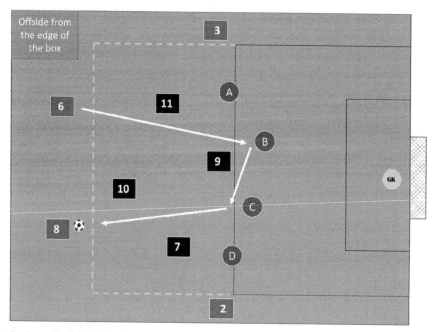

A bad pass by (6). Defenders must pass to the outside and they then become the attackers.

Transition Defending to Attacking

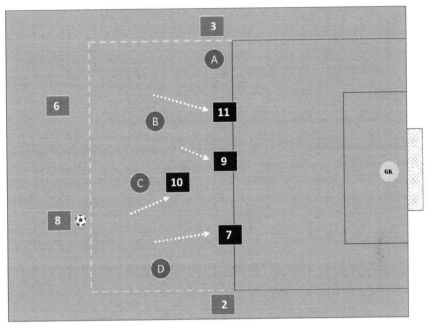

Helps to teach the front four how to defend effectively

Compare to Pressing in the Attacking Third

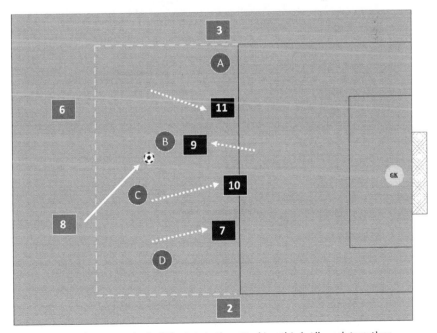

Now (9) presses the ball like it is in the attacking third. All work together.

Defending Principles

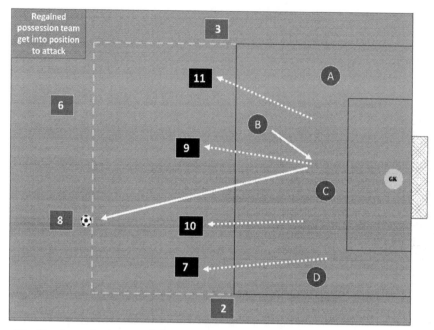

Attacking team give it away, defending team pass it out and get into position to attack.

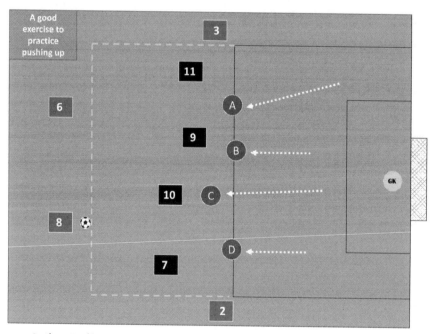

As the attacking team transition back, the defending team MUST push up also.

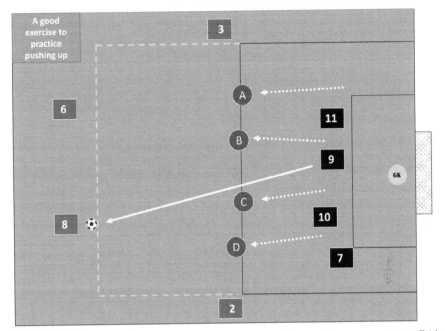

Exaggerated, but immediately the defending team must push up and leave opponents offside.

Angles of Support OFF the Ball Using Corridors

Rules:
a. A player can't pass straight forward in his own corridor or zone.
b. A player can pass forward to the other corridor.
c. A player can pass back in his own corridor.
d. Players have to pass diagonally forward because of the condition set. This develops the checking and passing habits of players.
e. Theme is to have them check off at an angle and sideways on so they can see the opponent, their team mates and the goal behind them.
f. We are using CONDITIONS to FORCE a THEME.
g. Quick passing and movement is desired so players must have great awareness and peripheral vision to make fast and accurate decisions in tight spaces.
h. This play can happen anywhere on the field, not just in the attacking third, so all players must have an awareness of how to position and move off the ball.

You can use this in any size game.

Players from both teams can move anywhere they like.

Develop:
*   You can play a straight pass forward through your own corridor if a player moves into it from another corridor.
*   If you pass it forward to an existing player in the same corridor then ultimately they receive the ball facing more or less backwards.
*   If you pass it straight forward to a player entering the same corridor then it is likely they are moving and facing forward as they receive the ball, which is what we are essentially trying to create.
*   To start, play unlimited touches, then 3 touches, then 2 touches and then one touch when it is on to do so.
*   Always encourage the players to think and act quickly.

The set up to promote angled support

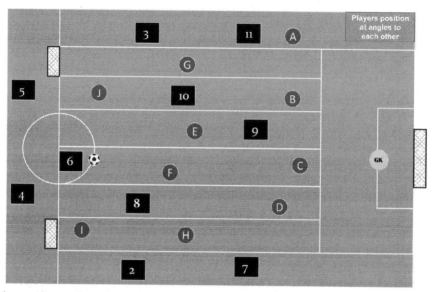

Eight corridors to play in. This teaches players to position to improve their PERIPHERAL VISION.
It might only be a case of a couple of yards, but it can be vital in terms of retaining the ball.
The CONDITION FORCES players to move and position correctly.

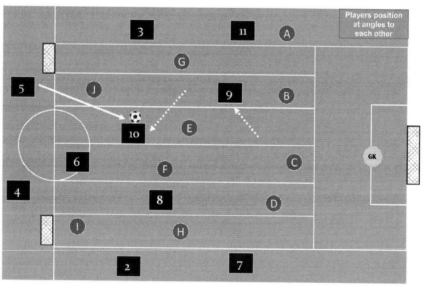

(10) cannot receive the pass in the same corridor so has to move into space and into an angled support
position. Now (10) receives the ball side on with better PERIPHERAL VISION, forward, back and to the side.
(9) then moves off the ball also to create angled support for (10) to pass.

Choices of pass

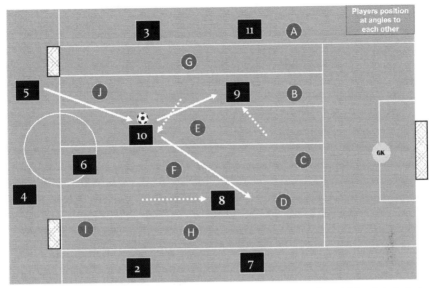

(10) is now in a much better position to use awareness instincts to see options. Ultimately (10) should try to position not only side on but ultimately facing forward on their first touch. Here (8) makes a good forward run, forming a natural angled position off the ball to receive.

Movements off the ball

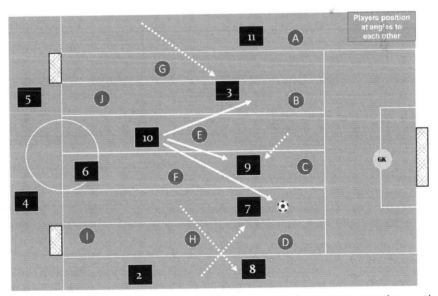

This set up also encourages wide players to make movements between zones as they use the coned lines as a guide. Using their own imagination, players will begin to interchange between zones and between each other so we get rotational movements.

Rotations and combination plays

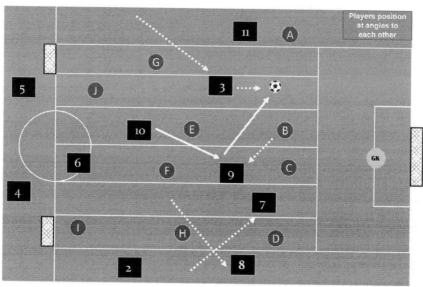

So now we have players dropping back to support and receive (getting free from markers) and moving forward to support and receive; rotations and combinations.

End product without showing recovery runs of defenders for clarity

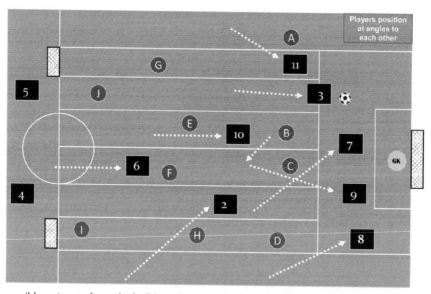

This is a possible outcome from the build up play. Quick passing and movement is desired, so players must have great awareness and peripheral vision to make fast decisions.

Movement from another corridor into the passing player's corridor

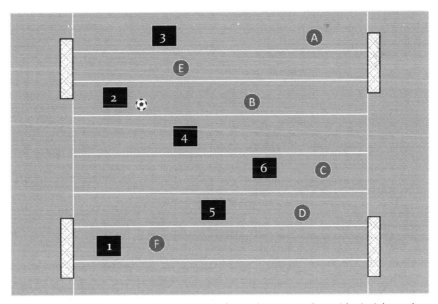

Good timing is essential here where the receiving player (9) times the run to accept the pass facing forward and not breaking stride in doing so. Therefore, the timing and weight of the pass has to be perfect too.

Using small goals and BOTH teams working on angled support: 6 v 6

Eight corridors to play in. A 6 v 6 game to small goals for each team. Each corridor is tight so the space for movements is constricted which forces players to position more intelligently OFF the ball.

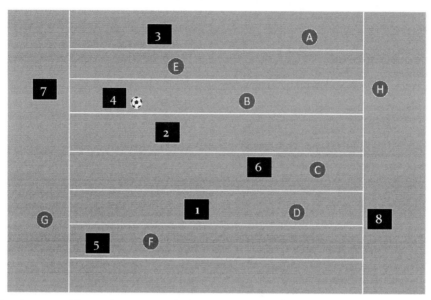

Pass and exchange positions to keep it going both ways. A directional practice with ANGLES OF SUPPORT as the primary theme. The corridors literally FORCE players to position off center and at an angle to the ball.

Training Using Corridors and Zones

For attacking and defending team shape:
Playing in 5 Corridors and 3 Zones using the 3-3-1-3

You can use this method of teaching with any system you like.

We divide the field up into Corridors and Zones to help players understand the major differences in spacing between attacking and defending team shape. We call them "Corridors" widthwise and "Zones" lengthwise. Below are some parameters to work off in my opinion. We first discuss the use of the Corridors.

Team Attacking Shape: Based on the 5 corridors width-wise we want all 5 to have players in them. Based length–wise we want a maximum of 2 of 3 zones filled; with the exception of the keeper.

Team Defending Shape: Based on the 5 corridors width-wise we want a maximum of 3 corridors filled with players, preferably 2.5 if possible.

Based length-wise we want a maximum of 2 of 3 zones filled. Preferably the whole team is condensed into 1.5 zones or at most half a field.

- Using Corridors is a great way to work out individual and collective field positioning as a team both offensively and defensively and it also gives players a real "focal point" to work off of.
- We use "Corridors" widthwise and then introduce "Zones" lengthwise later.
- These "focal points of reference" are a great way to teach players the differences between attacking and defending team shapes both widthwise and lengthwise.
- Particularly in defensive set-ups, it shows players how to mark in zones and how much tighter it should be than they will likely imagine and especially shows those players furthest from the ball defensively how important zonal marking is.
- Example, the ball is on our left with the other team and our right back is marking the opponent's opposite side winger far too wide. Having designated lines makes this much clearer.
- The theme is Positioning OFF the Ball as a Team
- This is a great session to help players identify positional variations. The 4 lines are used as a clear guide widthwise.
- Using such a fluid system of play as ours, putting the lines in as a condition is a great help.
- Example: if (7) goes outside (2) has to be inside (Phase 2 to Phase 3)
- Defining lines also forces players to play at angles to each other, thus improving their peripheral vision and their preferred side-on body shape.
- Divide the field in thirds lengthways also for attacking and defending principles to be worked on.
- High pressing is vital to allow us to push many players forward, so if we lose the ball in the attacking third we don't let them out.

Playing in 5 Corridors from a 3-3-1-3 widthwise

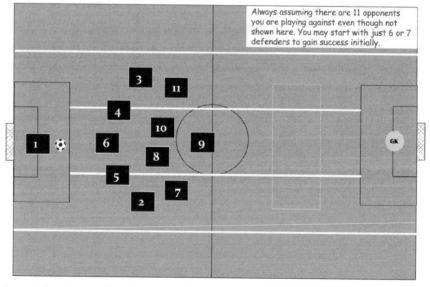

Playing in 5 corridors to help define the positioning of players. This is our starting position of 3-3-1-3. The keeper wins the ball and we change shape completely. This is Phase 1 of our 5 phases of play.

Playing in 5 Corridors from a 5-4-1 widthwise

This is our defending position of 5-4-1 possibly after recovering back and playing more defensively. The keeper wins the ball and we change shape completely.

Playing in 5 Corridors from a 3-3-1-3 widthwise

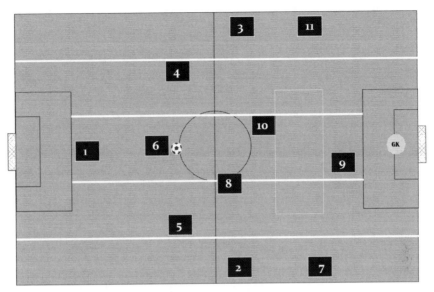

Here we have a good balance with players positioning at angles to each other.
This is Phase 2 of the 5 phases of play.

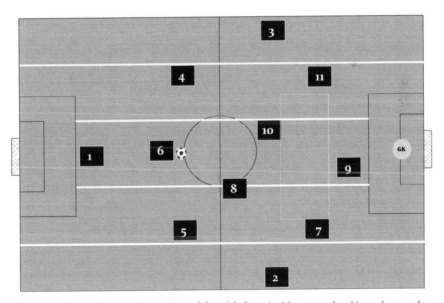

This is Phase 3 of the 5 phases of play where (7) and (11) cut inside to overload in and around zone 14.

Playing in 5 Corridors (3-3-1-3 / 3-4-3) widthwise

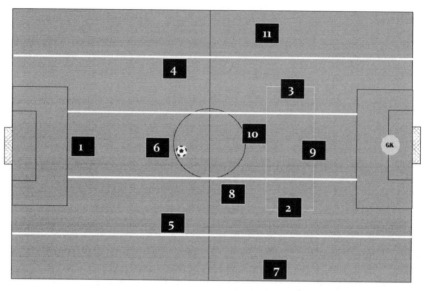

Now with wing fullbacks attacking inside in old fashioned inside forward positions, inside left and inside right. (7) and (11) maintain the width of the team. This is also Phase 3 of the 5 phases of play.

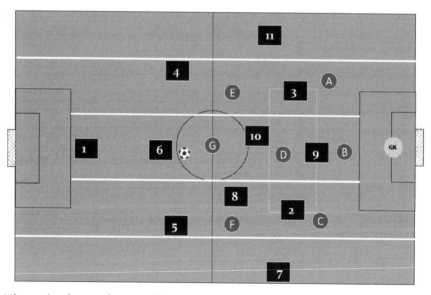

To start the session, have perhaps 7 or 8 opponents to play against to break the idea in gently and allow a chance of good success in terms of attacking team shape and maintaining possession of the ball. This is practicing rotational movements of players.

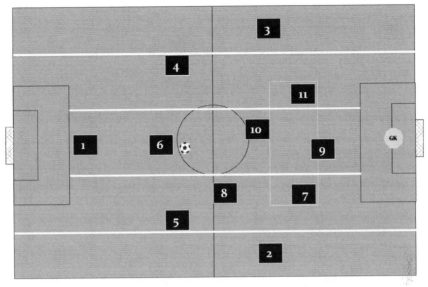

Now with wing fullbacks attacking outside with (7) and (11) in old fashioned inside forward positions, inside left and inside right. Wingbacks (2) and (3) maintain the width of the team.
This is Phase 3 of the 5 phases of play.

Playing in 5 Corridors (2-3-2-3)

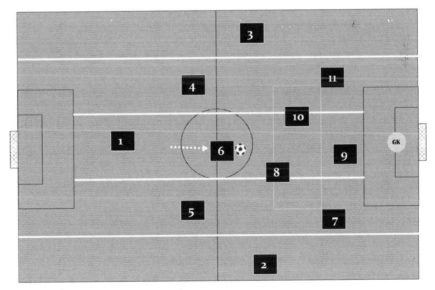

Playing in 5 zones to help define the positioning of players. Here we have a good balance with players positioning at angles to each other. (6) pushes forward to be the pivot or sweeper in front of the center backs.

Playing with 2 Pivots (2-2-3-3)

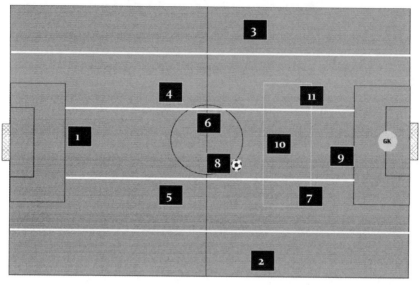

Here we play with 2 pivot players to ensure we are defensively tighter thru the middle. This takes good discipline and the team attacking shape is taken from the positioning of the 2 pivots who protect the back two center backs.

Playing with 2 Pivots (2-2-3-3): Defensive covering

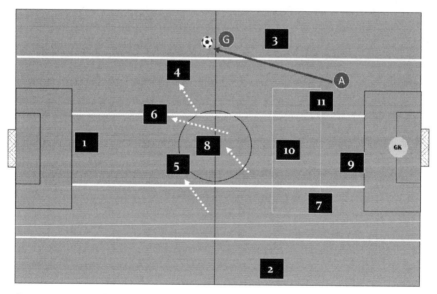

Let's say the opponents exploit the wide area which (3) has vacated to attack. Here is how our two pivot players are invaluable to cover for us to ensure defensive stability.

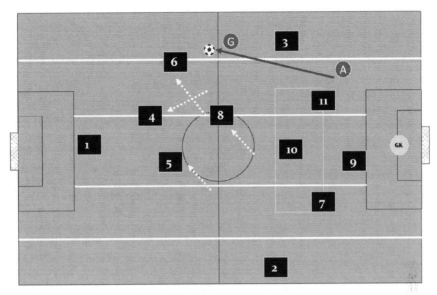

If (6) is closer he can press the player on the ball and (4) covers, (5) tightens closer to (4) and (8) condenses in front of the back three.

Playing with 2 Pivots (3-2-2-3)

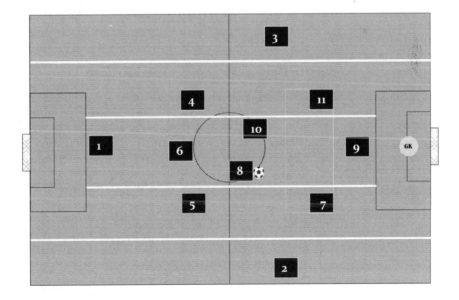

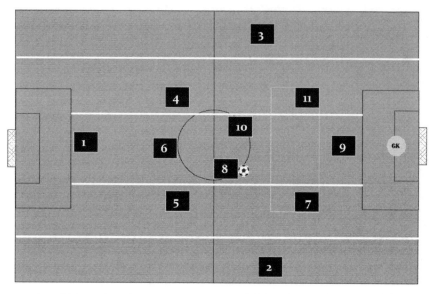

Here we play with two pivot players to ensure we are defensively tighter through the middle but with the security of three behind them, not just two. Example, we are winning but opponents are playing well so we add security.

Playing in 5 Corridors (2-1-4-3)

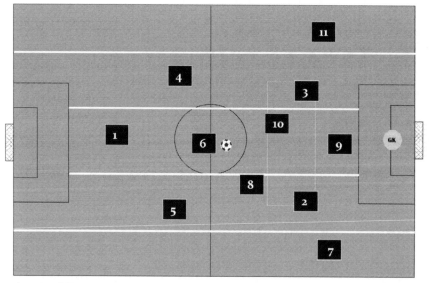

Here the wing fullbacks tuck in to gain superiority in numbers in midfield so should we lose it we win it back quickly and stop a possible counter attack. But (7) and (11) maintain the width for the team. Playing in inside left and inside right old fashioned positioning.

Defending against a counter attack from our attacking 2-1-4-3 set up using the "Corridors" concept

Stopping a counter attack (2-1-4-3)

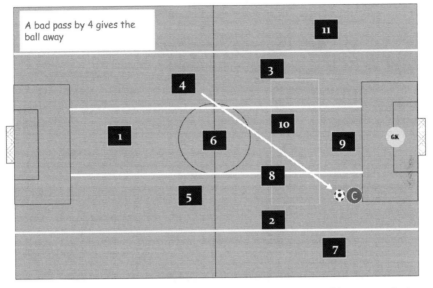

The idea here is to have a lot of players in attack so if we lose the ball we will have enough players close enough to stop a counter attack and win the ball back immediately. This is a very high pressing idea. The back two players are VERY high, even possibly in the opponent's half at some stage.

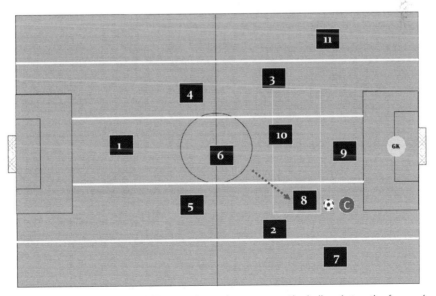

Wherever the ball is lost we should have a player close to press the ball and stop the forward pass because we allow so many to get into the attack. Other players must CONDENSE around the ball. (8) pressing and stopping forward motion allows them time to do this.

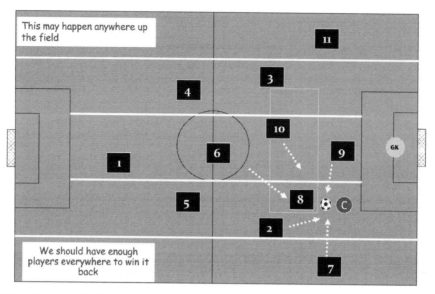

(8), (9) and (10) can do this now and we win the ball back immediately and start an attack on goal. (8) forces the opponent inside "if possible". Even (2) and (7) may join in. With many bodies forward we can stop the counter early so will not be exposed at the back. This saves a lot of chasing back also by putting the work in up front and close to goal.

Must be High Intensity Immediate Pressing

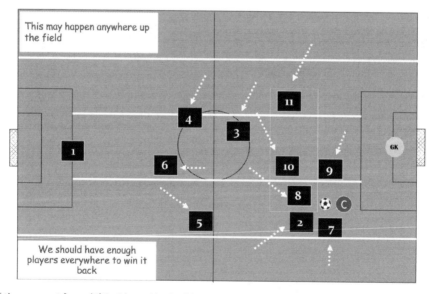

If they cannot force (C) inside and he is able to pass the ball forward (unlikely as it looks here), (5) has to anticipate this and react to it, in other words position channel side. (6) drops back for added security.

Example of changing Corridors: Simple rotation of (2) and (7)

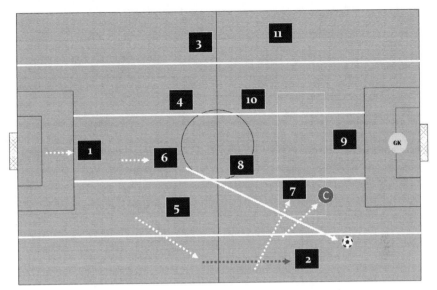

Now (7) cuts inside, clearing the space for (2) to overlap. (6) plays the ball into the space (7) has created for (2). This is phase 4 of the 5 Phases of play

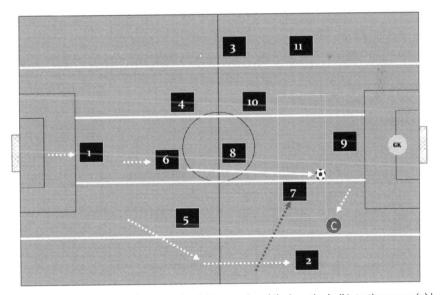

Now (7) cuts inside, clearing the space for (2) to overlap. (6) plays the ball into the space (7) has moved into from wide as defender (C) tracks (2)s run outside.

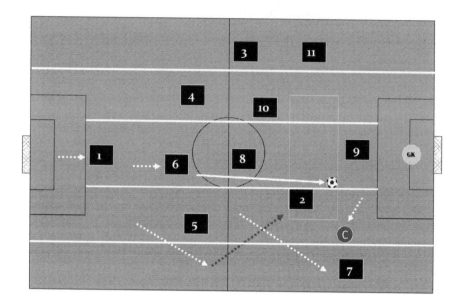

Setting Conditions to Establish Themes of Play
Using Corridors as a Guide

This does not at all mean that in the game it is wrong to play a forward pass in a straight line to a player. This can and will happen often. But it does get the players to "think" about supporting each other at angles OFF the ball to be in better position to potentially receive it.

Condition One:
a. Players CANNOT pass the ball forward in the same corridors so no one receives the ball facing backwards
b. All forward passes have to be at angles.
c. All support in front of the ball has to be at angles to the ball.
d. This encourages players to get side-on or facing forward when receiving the ball
e. Players CAN pass to the side or backwards in a straight line.

Condition Two:
a. Players CAN pass forward in the same corridor but ONLY if a player runs into it from a DIFFERENT corridor as the ball arrives so he is facing forward as he receives it and running onto it.
b. Now players can interchange to create space for each other, which should pose problems for marking opponents.
c. Just by setting this condition players HAVE to move to receive the ball if the pass is in a straight line going forward.

Set a Condition to Establish a Theme

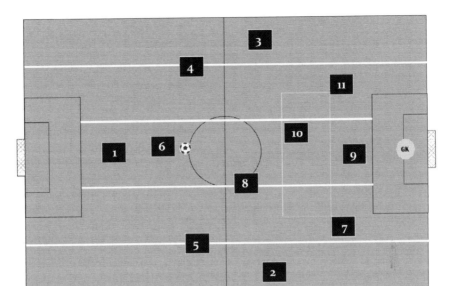

Now the players CANNOT pass the ball forward in the same corridors so no one receives the ball facing backwards. Every pass forward is at an angle, but players can pass to the side or backwards in a straight line.

Condition 1 to force an angled passing theme

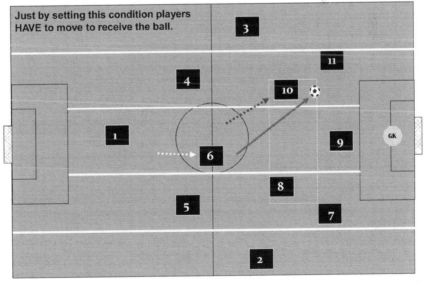

Now the players CANNOT pass the ball forward in the same corridor so no one receives the ball facing backwards. This will get players to position at angles to each other to receive the ball and try to get at least side on to have a greater peripheral vision of the field. Here (10) moves to be able to receive the ball.

Condition 2 to allow a straight pass

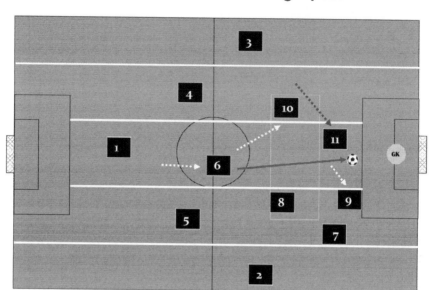

New Condition: you can pass forward in the same corridor if a player runs into it as the ball arrives so they are facing forward and running as they receive it.

Condition 2: almost forces players to rotate and interchange positions

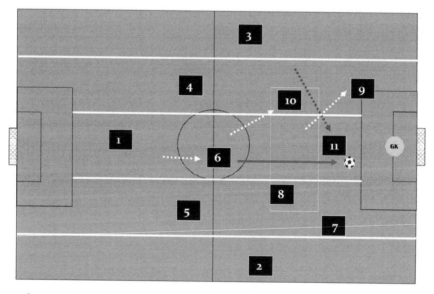

Now players can interchange to create space for each other, which should pose problems for marking opponents. Just by setting this condition players HAVE to move to receive the ball.

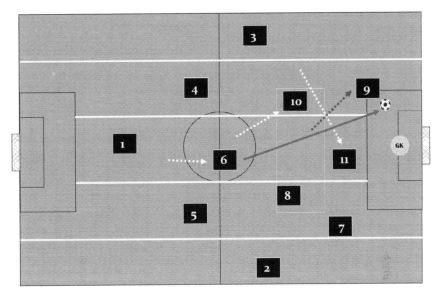

(6) could also pass to (9) if he has gotten free. We can develop 2, 3 and 4 player rotations from this one idea / condition.

Another idea using the set condition

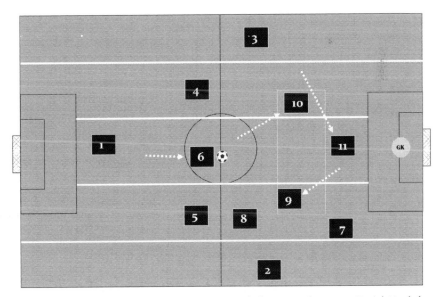

Example; (6) on the ball can play to three potential players on the move. Straight to (11) as (11) has moved from a different corridor or to (9) or (10) as they have moved away from the straight pass into a different corridor.

Adding ZONES lengthwise to the field

Up to now we have used "Corridors" to divide the field up widthwise and now we look at the "length" of the field. We add 3 "Zones" to divide the field up (you can use 4 zones if you like).

Team Attacking: Based lengthwise now, we want a maximum of 2 of 3 zones filled; with the exception of the keeper.

Team Defending: Based lengthwise we want a maximum of 2 of 3 zones filled. Preferably, the whole team is condensed into 1.5 zones; or at most half a field.

Changing from attacking to defensive team shape

Defensive team shape often begins from losing the ball from an attacking team shape (and vice – versa) so we need to set up from that starting point to practice winning the ball back. In other words, we don't necessarily set up from a 3-3-1-3, with four units of 4, 5 and 6, then 8, then 2, 3 and 10 and finally up top 7, 9 and 11.

The 4 units of the 3-3-1-3 team can be composed of different players based on the adventure and freedom of the team. 3-3-1-3 attacking shape is 4,5,6; then 8, then 2,3,10, then 7,9 and 11. But it could, for example, be 4,5,8; 6, then 7,10,11, and finally up front 2,3; and 9. Or MANY other permutations.

Attacking: Based on the 5 corridors widthwise we want all 5 corridors to have players in them. Based lengthwise we want a maximum of 2 of 3 zones filled; with the exception of the keeper.

Defending: Based on the 5 corridors widthwise we want a maximum of 3 corridors filled with players, preferably 2.5 if possible. Based length-wise we want a maximum of 2 of 3 zones filled, preferably the whole team is condensed into 1.5 zones or at most half a field.

Using Shadow play for initial understanding

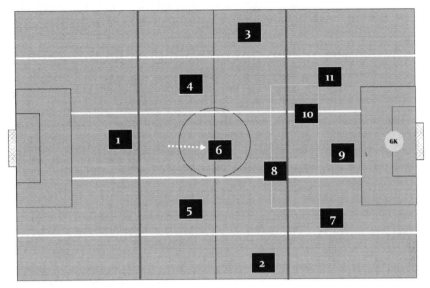

Play without opponents and show our basic attacking shape, then offer alternatives for pressing as a group and have them do it as fast as possible. No ball needed but I will add it in the next diagrams for clarity.

Using Shadow play

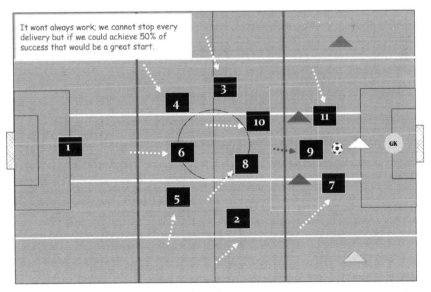

Play without opponents and show our basic attacking shape, then offer alternatives for pressing as a group and have them do it as fast as possible. Use different color cones to represent where we lost the ball, then organize the team around this defensive starting point with the players deciding where they think they should be and why.

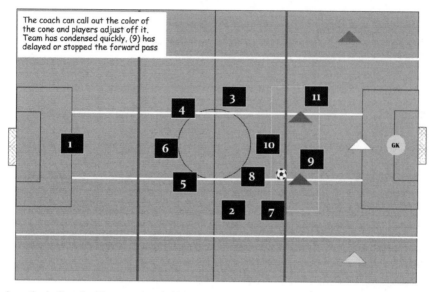

If we lose the ball at the blue cone, we adjust as shown. (8) MUST slow down the player in an actual game to allow time for this to happen.

You can extend this back to the middle third also

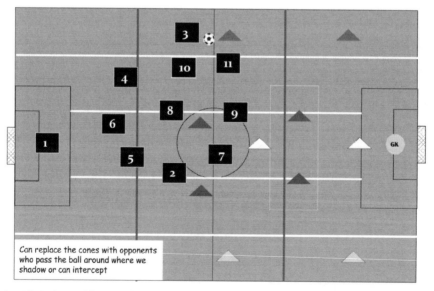

We lose it wide in the middle third (indicated by the ball in the diagram). Try to press them inside to where our strength is in numbers. Wing full backs have to be brave and stay in midfield but condense in. (3) delays and shows inside to (10), the rest condense. (10) cuts off the passing lane forward as does (11) inside or back. It will NEVER be this picture perfect but this shows what we should strive for. Pivot (6) is the key for cover.

Dividing the field into fifths widthwise and thirds lengthwise

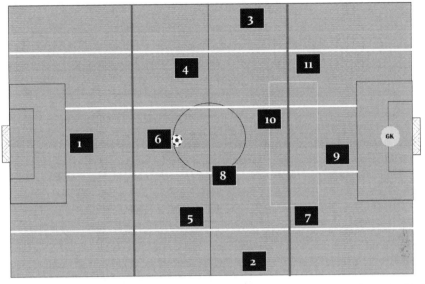

Playing in five corridors widthwise to help define the positioning of players. Also playing in thirds from goal to goal lengthwise (lets call these ZONES for clarity). Here we have a good balance with players positioning at angles to each other. We must get the team into two thirds only, except for the keeper, both offensively and defensively.

Too spread out from goal to goal

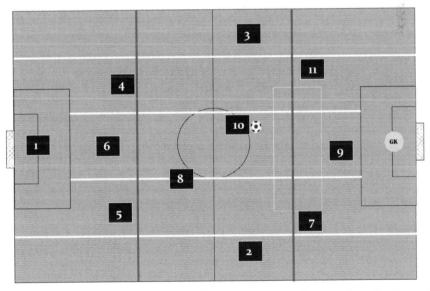

Our team is too big with too much space to allow for a counter attack. So even when attacking we have to think about what to do if we lose it. Players are spread out in three zones. On the other hand if you don't want to risk being caught high defensively with a ball in behind then you may set up deeper like this. But it isn't my way to play.

We become a 3-4-3 or 3-1-3-3 if (8) or (10) drops back a little

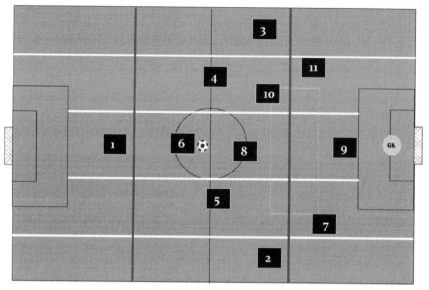

This is what our attacking team shape will look like with wing fullbacks now in midfield or they could even join the front three due to the fluidity of our way of playing. Players are condensed into two zones except for the keeper.

Playing a Pressing game comes from the back

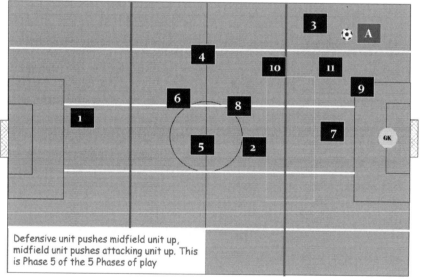

Defensive unit pushes midfield unit up, midfield unit pushes attacking unit up. This is Phase 5 of the 5 Phases of play

If we want to play a pressing game then we must have the back three as high as possible and then the responsibility of the front players is to press as soon as possible when we lose it to stop a counter attack. Same in midfield where we now have our wing fullbacks positioned.

Defensive set up with wing fullbacks pushed on

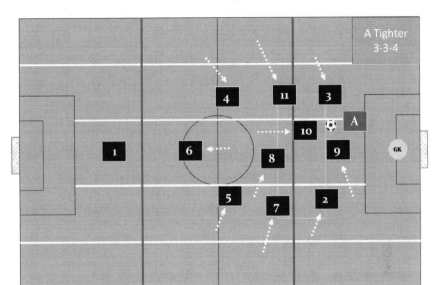

Now we see the immediate pressing players are the highest up the field as we just lost the ball there. In this case it's the wing full backs and striker (9). This is an example where we lose the ball outside their box but immediately press to win it back.

Wing Full Backs on the offensive

This is what our attacking team shape will look like with wing fullbacks now in attack due to the freedom we allow where they are clearly covered defensively in this set up. This teaches players how to immediately set up defensively from attacking positioning with many players high but with organized cover behind.

Fast Defensive alteration overloading central midfield

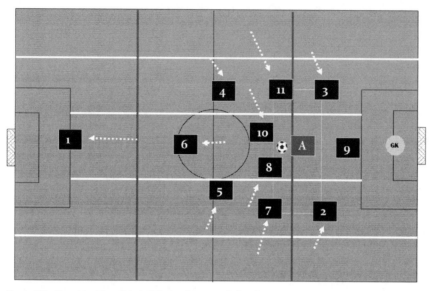

We lose the ball in the attacking third. This is what our defending team shape will look like with all players except (6) and the keeper now tucked inside in midfield. (6) and the keeper drop to guard against the long ball. If opponents play wide we immediately slide wide as a team.

Observations on quick pressing

It won't always work. We cannot stop every delivery from the opponents trying to get in behind us because we defend high, but if we could achieve 50% success that would be a great start.

50% success means in 30 deliveries we get 15 successful immediate wins back. This saves a a lot of recovery running and energy used, plus we are in a great position to attack.

If we allow the forward pass, the whole team will be forced to recover back various distances depending on their position. Plus, when we next win it back we will be in a much poorer position from which to attack. Additionally, we lose territorial advantage.

SO, stop it at the SOURCE. A short and immediate 5 to 10 yard burst by one player to press and delay (or win) the ball can save 50 yard runs for others. But we need this same burst from 3 or 4 players collectively to be really effective.

So 15 deliveries stopped means a saving for midfield players of 15 x 50 yards, potentially over 750 yards of speed and high and vital energy not used up. And that number only gets higher with increased successes.

Therefore, the closest and next closest players to the ball when it is lost MUST switch on immediately from an offensive to defensive mentality to win or delay. This is vital for success!

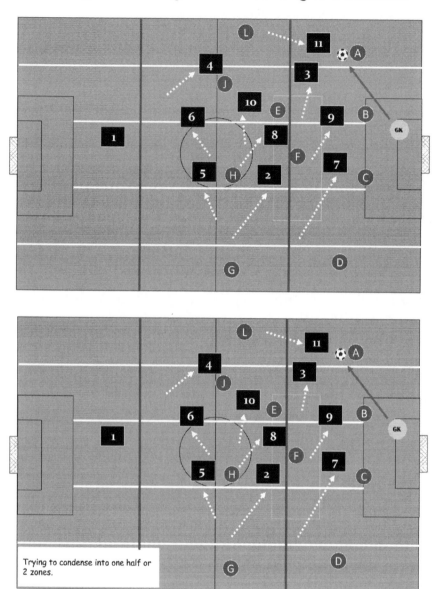

Pressing in attacking third condensing to 3 corridors

Trying to condense into one half or 2 zones.

Condensing the spaces close to the ball. (11) forces (A) inside to the support and blocks the pass to (I). (3) is already up there and so is the next pressing player. Don't worry about (D) and (G) and (4) already has covered the space should (A) be able to play the ball long. Defending just inside our own half.

The ball is played in behind the opponents

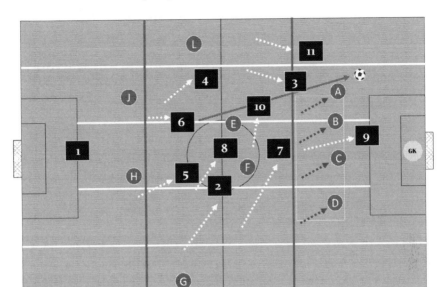

The ball is played in behind the opponent's back four and we MUST press immediately to stop (A) getting to the ball and turning to play forward. (9) cuts off the back pass to the keeper. Also press up from the back.

Pressing in attacking third condensing to 3 corridors

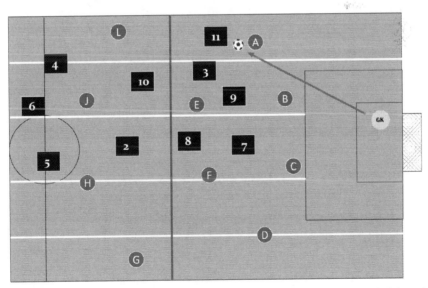

Defensive set up. Everyone condensed into 3 corridors wide or less (more like 2.5 wide). (9) can be ready for the back pass to (B) or the keeper, (7) can be ready for the change of play to (C) or (D), almost inviting (A) to pass back so we can press quickly in front of goal. We MUST stop the forward pass.

The ball is played in behind the opponents

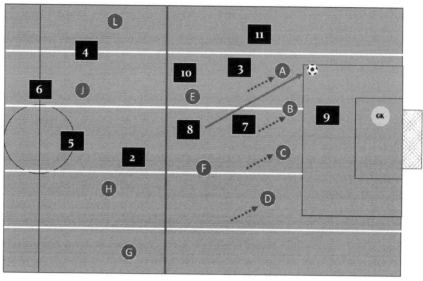

(9) prevents the back pass. (A) is favorite for the ball but we can stop (A) from controlling and turning and passing. A great place to win the ball and attack the goal.

Attacking in the attacking third opening to 5 corridors

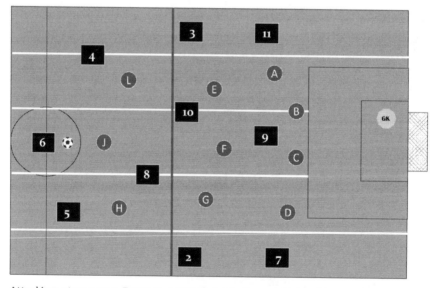

Attacking set up 3-3-1-3. Everyone opened up into five corridors wide, opening up spaces between opponents and making it much harder to defend against. Players position between opponents to get into open passing lanes.

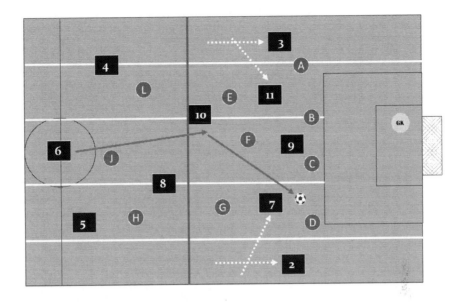

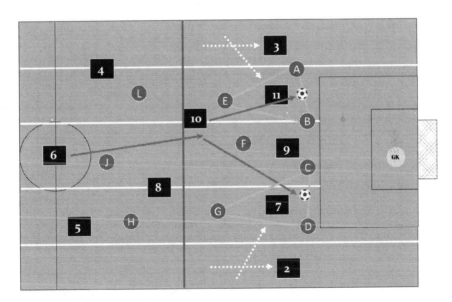

(7) and (11) position between opponents to find the best spaces to receive. (2) and (3) distract (A) and (D). (11) positions in the middle of (A), (B) and (E). (7) positions in-between (D), (G) and (C).

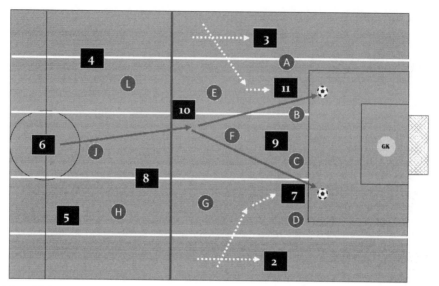

If (A) and (D) track us wide with (7) and (11) this will allow them to cut back inside into the space they have created for themselves. We can play the ball between and behind them.

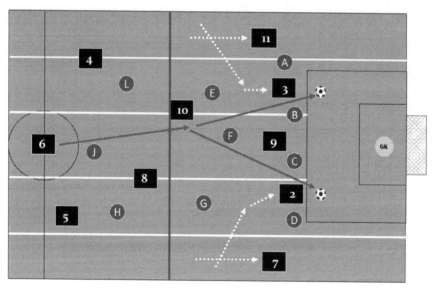

It could be (2) and (4) who cut inside to attack also. This is far less predictable and might catch opponents out.

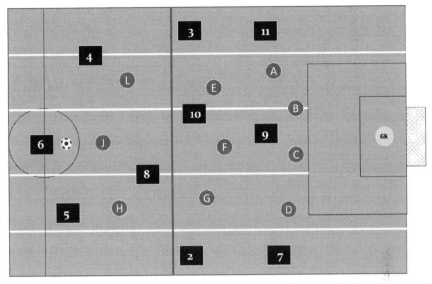

Attacking set up 3-3-1-3. We want players to move between corridors to interchange and rotate to fool and confuse the opposition, making sure we have at least one player in each corridor.

Dividing the field into fifths widthwise and quarters lengthwise

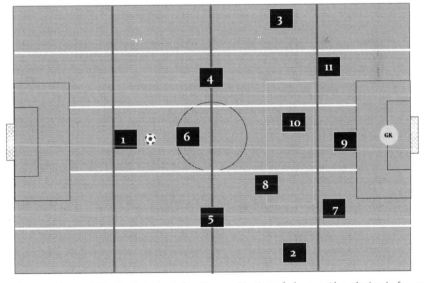

Playing in five corridors widthwise to help define the positioning of players. Also playing in four quarters from goal to goal lengthwise (lets call these ZONES for clarity). Here we have a good balance with players positioning at angles to each other. We must get the team into 2 to 2.5 quarters only, except for the keeper, both offensively and defensively.

Playing Against Different Systems

Playing a 5-4-1 when pressured and then Counter Attacking

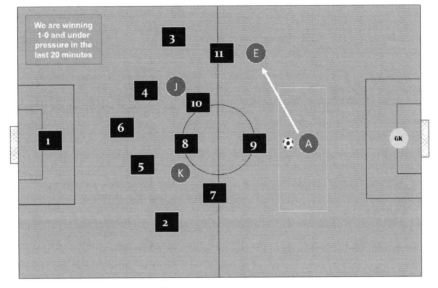

We are under immense pressure from the opponent's full team press. We drop (6) into a sweeper role. Our counter attack policy is to hit (7), (9) or (11) early and support quickly.

A 3-3-1-3 against a 4-3-1-2

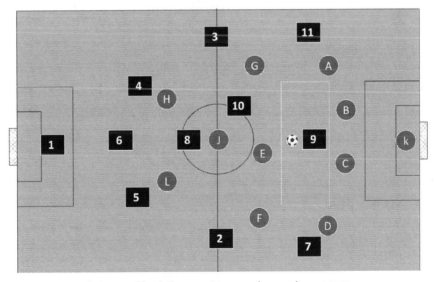

But a zonal back three, not two markers and a sweeper.

3-3-1-3 becoming an attacking 2-3-2-3 against a 4-3-1-2

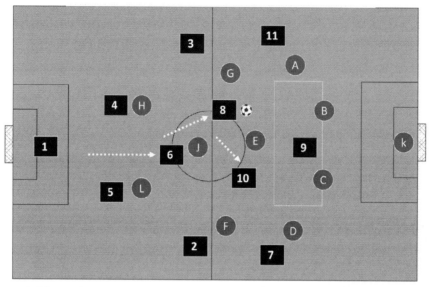

We can push (6) onto their attacking midfield player and release (8). When we lose possession, (6) can drop in behind the two center backs and (8) can drop back to pick up the attacking midfielder.

3-3-1-3 becoming an attacking 2-3-2-3 against a 4-2-3-1

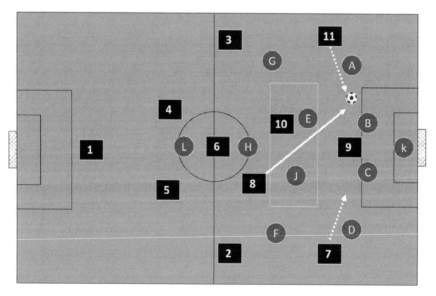

Now we can overload the center of midfield and (7) and (11) can position "between" the opponent's defenders in "no man's land". This allows space wide for (2) and (3).

We need a Plan B or C

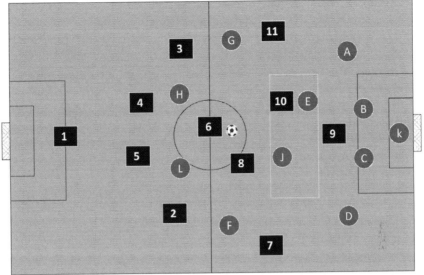

Here is our usual start position set up. Depending on the moment (and score) in the game we may need to look to change our original set up. This we should practice in training to prapare the players.

Changing Game Strategy and systems / style of play to suit the moment / score in the game situation

These are some basic ideas to think over and consider. We cannot cover every eventuality but this will give food for thought. We can work on these in coaching clinics or you can do it in your own training to ensure your players are prepared. Every coach's input is important and if we come up with a better plan through a collective discussion, even better.

It is important to have at least one option to use for each situation going into a game; and practiced on the training field so players fully understand what is required when the situation occurs. We are looking to develop the balance between development of the players and also having a winning formula to base it on.

Situation #1: When in a winning position with let's say 20 minutes to go and under intense pressure, we must try to kill off the game by playing "percentages in safety and risk" areas of the field and in the game. It may be "ugly" to watch but it is a major part of being successful; being able to change your Game Strategy to suit the moment.

Strategies:
1. We will not attempt to play so purely from the back as may be the norm and put ourselves under pressure by losing the ball in dangerous areas, unless we have plenty of time in that moment.

2. We may try to slow the "tempo" of the game down and break the rhythm of the opponents, which in itself may be a change in strategy within the overall game strategy.

3. We may decide to play long balls into our striker and by-pass our midfield and then look to support him from behind instead of playing our usual controlled short passing game. We may substitute our short, fast striker for a bigger and stronger striker who will hold the ball up better to suit this new game strategy.

4. We may defend much deeper than usual and use a counter attacking policy on regaining possession.

5. The opponents are pressing high up the field so on regaining possession we will play the ball in behind their defense "immediately" to first get them turned and then press high ourselves OR, use this to give us time to reorganize defensively, remain deep and keep our defensive shape unless a clear counter is on.

6. Play a short corner and keep the ball.

Each game presents a new unique problem we have to solve. These are some suggestions as to what we can do to ensure we win the game.

Situation #2: When in a losing position with 20 minutes to go and under intense pressure, we must try to get back into the game by taking calculated risks or even throwing caution to the wind to chase the game.

Strategies:

1. We leave three players up at all times with NO defensive responsibilites. This means that when we defend we may get overloaded, but once we regain the ball we have three immediate targets in very advanced positions on the field to hit the ball to quickly.

2. We defend very high up the field and play a heavy and high pressing game from back to front to try to win the ball back in the attacking third.

3. We play 2 or 3 at the back to get more players forward and in attacking start positions, leaving us prone to a counter attack perhaps, but we must get back into the game.

4. We play long in behind the opponents to get the ball in the attacking third quickly and get the opponents turned and maintain the pressure.

5. We substitute defensive players for more attacking minded players to suit the occasion and give them free license to attack.

As previously, these are just suggestions to consider. You may see different solutions per the situation.

It is always good to spend time in training working on different scenarios such as these to get the players more familiar and comfortable and thus more relaxed about them in an actual game. They will obviously play better when relaxed than when in a panic when these situations occur in live games, as they inevitably will.

We are losing with 20 minutes to go; we can play 2-3-2-3 permanently (with #6 as security)

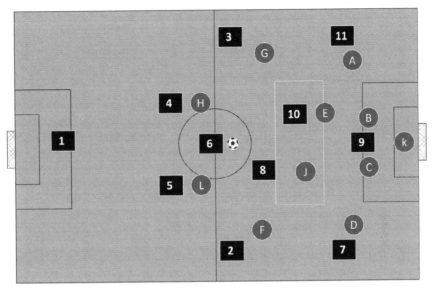

We gamble 2 v 2 at the back. We lose possession and (6) immediately drops back into a sweeper role. The 2-3-2-3 is the "attacking formation" of the 4-2-3-1 so the transition to this as a "start position" should be easy for the players to understand.

We are winning with 20 minutes to go and under intense pressure; we can play a 5-4-1 against a 4-4-2

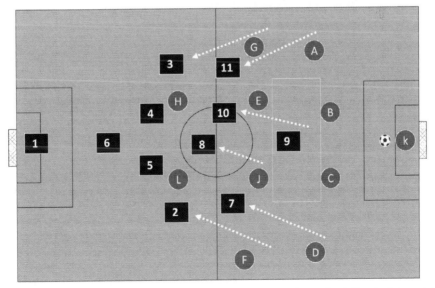

Our two fullbacks (2) and (3) take up very defensive positions to form a back five. (10) drops into a midfield four. Back four stay intact. Counter attack through (7), (9), (10) and (11).

Opponents could do this?

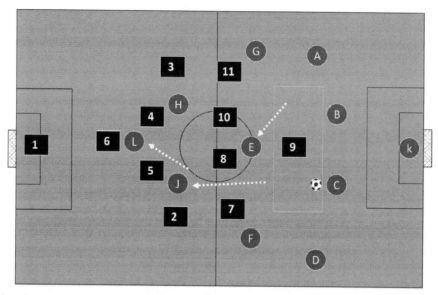

Push a player onto the sweeper to put him under pressure. It is important now that (6) steps up to leave the opponent offside as often as he can. What else could we do to counter this?

Or this:

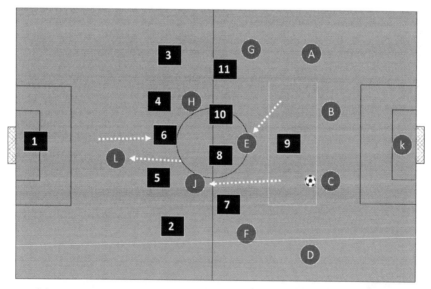

Here (6) steps up to leave the opponent offside. What else could we do to counter this?

We are down to ten men with 20 minutes to go against a 4-3-3 and we are winning, we set up in a 5-3-1

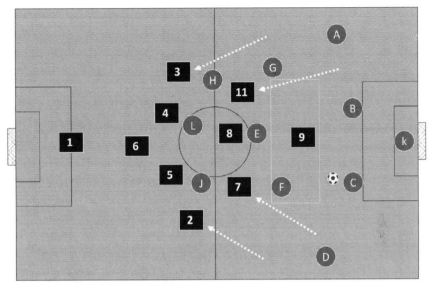

We even it up in midfield 3 v 3 and have a 5 v 3 advantage at the back.
Counter attack through (7), (9) and (11).

We are down to ten men with 20 minutes to go against a 4-4-2 and we are winning; we set up in a 4-4-1

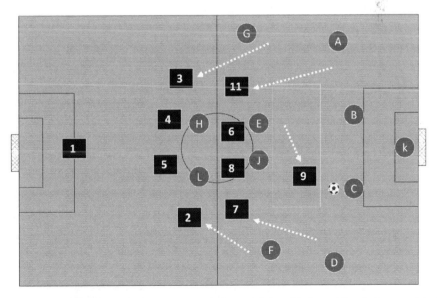

We even it up in midfield 4 v 4 and counter attack through (7) and (11) providing fast support to (9).
(9) must be able to hold the ball up until he gets support.

We are down to ten men with 20 minutes to go against a 4-4-2 and we are losing; we set up in a 4-2-3 (2-4-3)

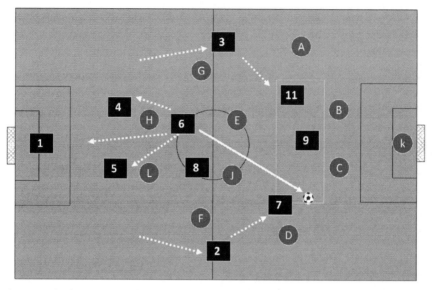

Match 2 v 2 in the center of midfield and attack through the three strikers. (6) and (8) protect the center backs, (6) can drop in to cover when needed. We attack through fullbacks and wide strikers (7) and (11) to support (9). Try to create a 3 v 2 against the opponent's 2 center backs.

We are down to ten men with 20 minutes to go against a 4-4-2 and we are losing; we set up in an offensive 4-2-3 (2-4-3) but push both wing backs on

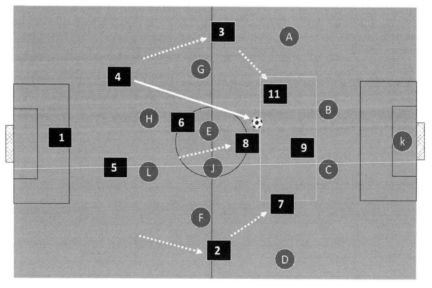

We could really go for it and try to fill in the #10 position and see what the opponents do (if they see it?). A big gamble perhaps, but we are losing!!

We are down to ten men with 20 minutes to go against a 3-5-2 and we are losing; we set up in an offensive 4-2-3 (2-4-3)

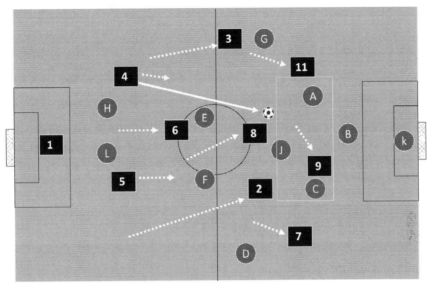

Not showing the movements of opponents for clarity. Obviously, they will react to our movements, but if we do them quickly perhaps we will get a step on them. Go 3 v 3 up top.

We are down to ten men with 20 minutes to go against a 3-5-2 and we are losing; we set up in an offensive 4-2-3 (2-4-3)

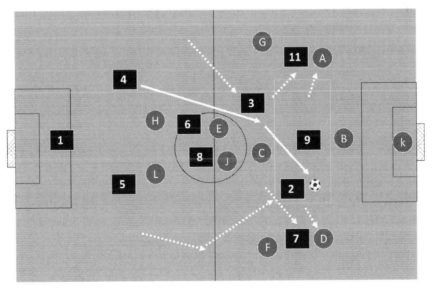

We go 2 v 2 against them at the back. Test them by going 2 wide and one central to see if they man mark and track the runner, then attack inside as shown. This is unlikely, but you never know.

We are down to ten men with 20 minutes to go against a 3-5-2 and we are losing; we set up in an offensive 4-2-3 (2-4-3)

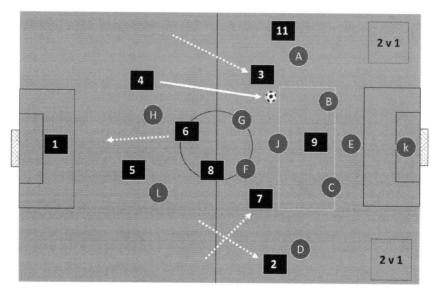

We go 3 v 3 against them at the back. Test them by going 2 wide and one central. If they mark the inside "zones" then attack wide in a 2 v 1 on each side. This is more likely.

Common Problems and How to Fix Them

Certain things happen in games too often for them not to be a one off or a coincidence. I have identified several that I have come across consistently with my teams over the years and I am assuming you may come across them too and have a need to focus upon them and put them right.

1. Dropping then Pressing
2. Do we drop or press up from the back?
3. Not closing the wide player down
4. Not pressing the ball from a clearance
5. Not pressing the striker all the way
6. Allowing opponent midfield players to receive and turn
7. NOT Sliding across and changing who you mark
8. We defend too deep from free kicks
9. They get the ball out and keep possession; we have to press and also recover at the same time
10. We don't press together as a unit in the Attacking Third
11. We lose the ball with a bad pass: This has happened too much where we get countered
12. Wide players do not recover leaving a 2 v 1 against

1. Dropping then Pressing

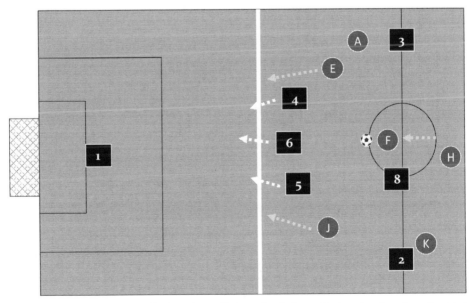

Opponents attack us centrally. Defenders drop off more slowly than attackers to allow them to get closer. We want to drop only so far then shout "STEP UP" and we collectively step up and press the ball.

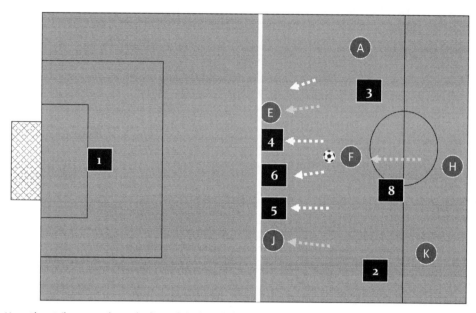

Here the strikers are along the line of the last defender, that is the instance the 3 central defenders step and leave them offside and press the ball together.

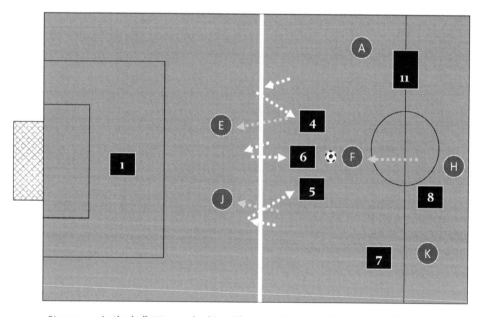

Step up – win the ball. We can do this with 2 or 3 players as the last line of defense.

Offside runs result from our pressing

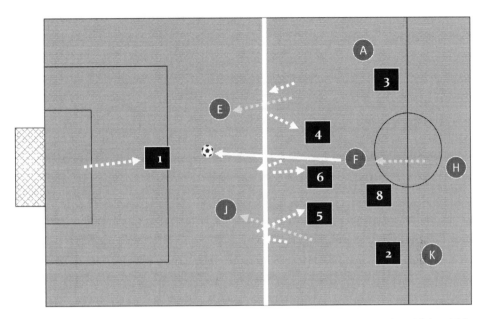

(F) manages to pass the ball beyond the back three. The ball is passed through and (E) and (J) are CLEARLY offside. Keeper sweeps up.

Win the ball, start an attack

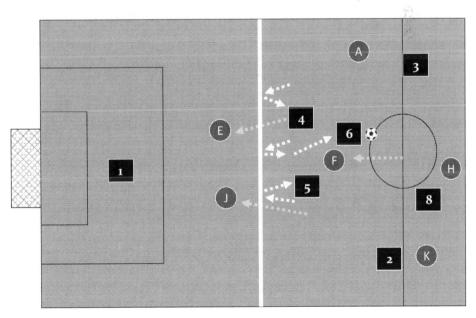

Either (4), (5) or preferably (6) MUST win the ball or (F) will be through on goal. Here (6) wins it and starts an attack. Having three players to close down one player is a big advantage and should be used.

Same with a through pass

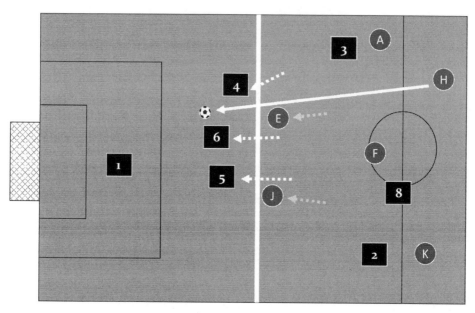

(4), (5) and (6) MUST DROP. One of the center backs has to be a GREAT COMMUNICATOR. Watch the player on the ball and his body language and if there is NO pressure on the ball we drop as shown.

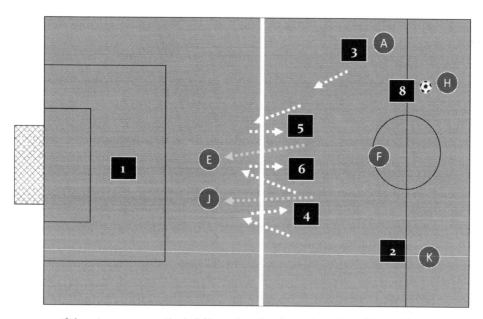

If there is pressure on the ball (from 8) and we know it can't be delivered but strikers are still running forward, the call is STEP UP and we let them run offside. COMMUNICATION is the KEY again.

2. Do we drop or press up from the back?

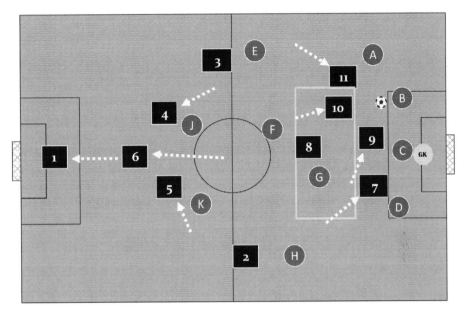

While the front players attack, the back players can drop off and guard against a counter attack IN ANTICIPATION of the ball being played behind us.

We could set up like this

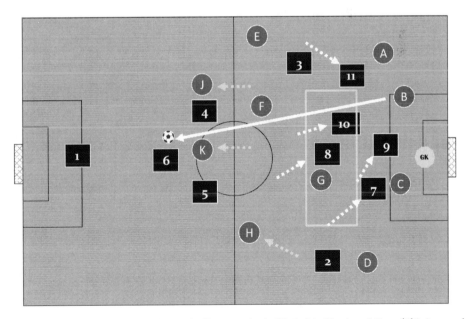

We always have the center backs dropped off in case the ball in behind is played. Here (6) is in a perfect position to cover. This is (6)'s Start Position.

This is what we could do also

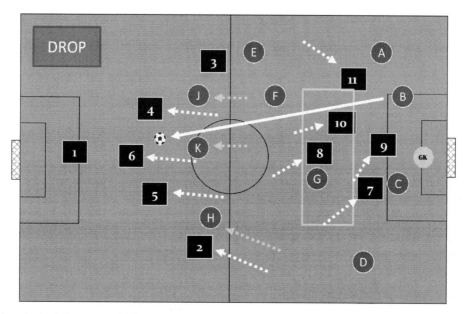

Based on the body language of (B) looking to play the ball long, (4), (5) and (6) drop off BEFORE the delivery. When the ball IS played forward they are in good defensive positions.

Full Team Press

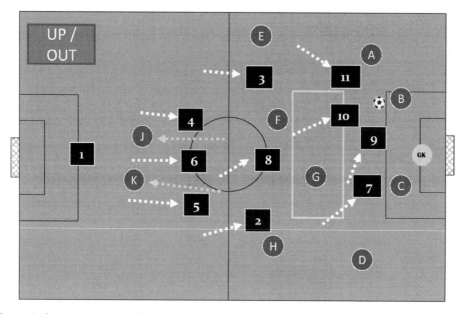

Alternatively we may press up from the back, leaving opponents offside should they get a chance of a counter attack. Defenders must decide in a split second which course of action they take.
AND THEY MUST TALK!!

3. Not closing the wide player down

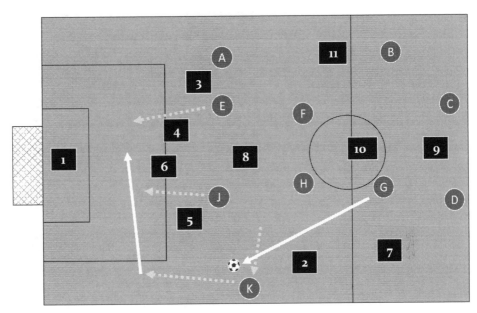

We allow players to get the ball and face us too many times, creating 1 v 1's in their favor which result in too many crosses into the box. Here, (K) runs wide wingback (2) allows him to get behind and (5) doesn't press.

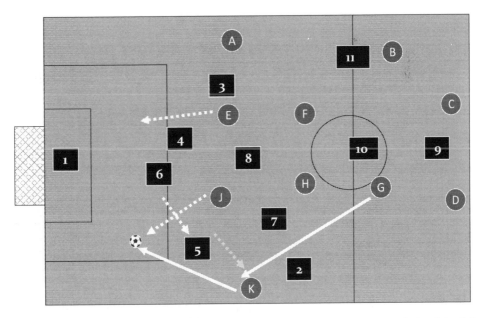

Alternatively with (K) receiving and facing forward he cannot be stopped from passing behind the defense into striker (J), causing more problems.

Closing the wide player down

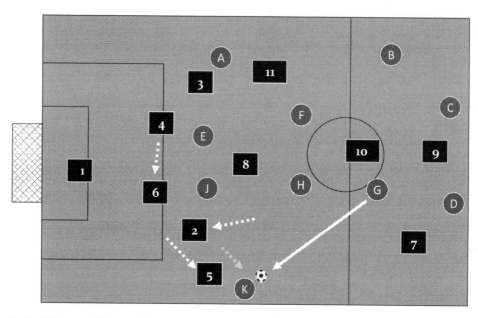

Defender (2) closes (K) down who now has to receive the ball facing back. There is no danger of a cross coming in from this position. Timing of the run by (5) is vital here as is "jockeying / delaying" and not diving in. This allows (2) to recover and help. Don't allow (K) to receive and turn and face up.

4. Not pressing the ball from a clearance

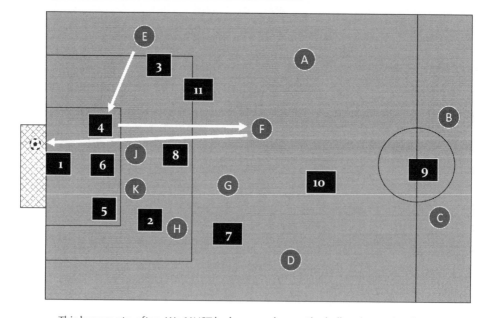

This happens to often. We MUST be brave and press the ball and stop the shot.

This is what should happen

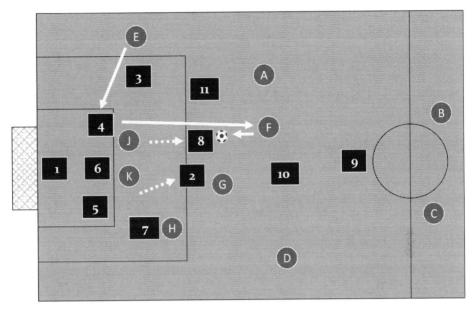

Immediately as the ball is headed clear, (8) must be tight to (F) to stop the shot, as should (2) to (G) so no one is free for the 2nd ball clearance.

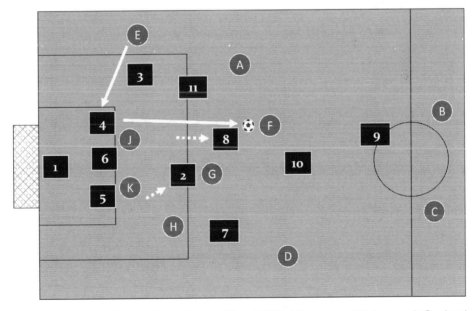

Better still, (8) and (2) should be picking up (F) and (G) tightly anyway. This is so easily fixed and will keep us from conceding VERY UNNECESSARY cheap goals.

This is what ultimately should happen

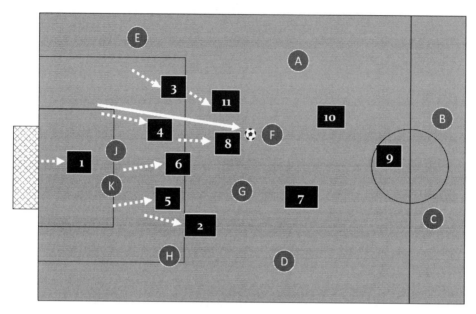

Here the defense pushes out "as the ball travels", leaving opponents offside. We may even have a counter on should (8) win the ball. WE NEED TALKERS TO GET UP AND OUT.

5. Not pressing the striker all the way

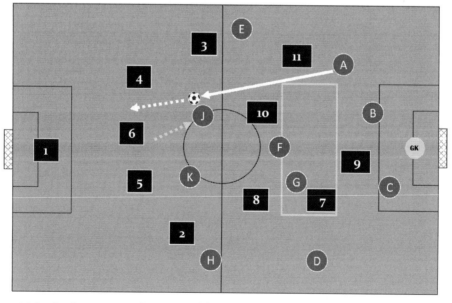

Another mistake that happens too often. Striker (J) checks back to receive to feet and center back (6) allows it. (J) receives and turns and runs at the defense, leaving us vulnerable in a 1 v 1.

Now pressing the striker all the way

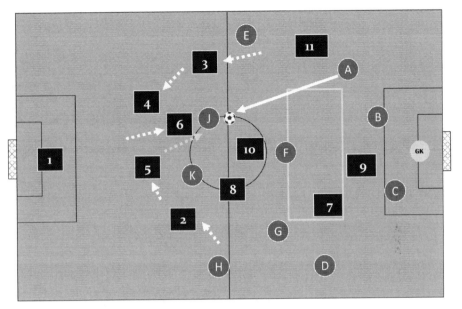

Now defender (6) is in charge (he could even try to intercept and start an attack). Striker (J) has his back to goal instead of facing forward running at (6).

Opponent Striker goes really deep

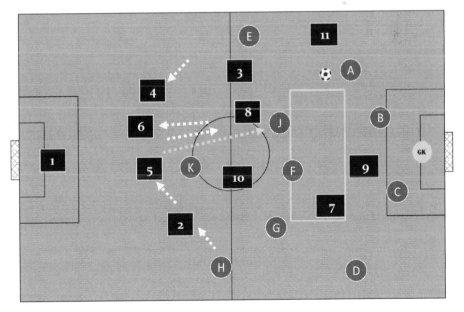

Alternatively if the striker goes really deep then PASS HIM ON to a midfield player and drop back into the back four. But TALK, tell the midfielder the striker is coming. Here (8) now picks him up, he is little danger to us from here.

6. Allowing opposing midfield players to receive and turn

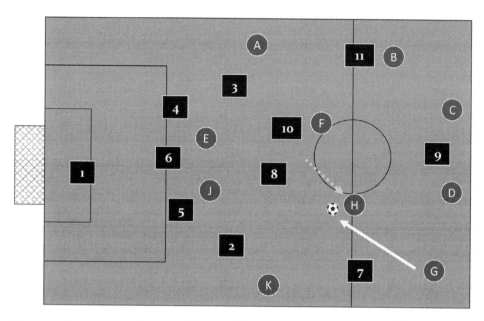

Seems an obvious one and is easy to fix. Here (H) comes short to receive a pass from a defender. (8) does not close down this player and allows him to receive and turn and attack us.

Such a simple solution that isn't always done

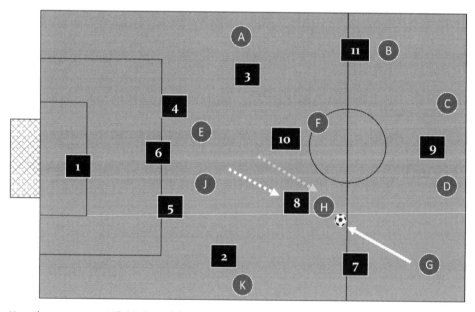

Here, because our midfield player (8) has made the effort to close down (H), he has saved a lot of work for his teammates.

7. NOT Sliding across and changing who you mark

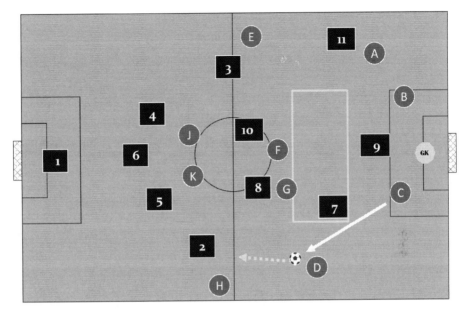

Another common one where they outnumber us in an area. (7) is out of position and (D) is now free. (8) is marking (G) and is afraid to leave him. So (D) has a free run at (2), creating a 2 v 1 with (H).

This is what should happen

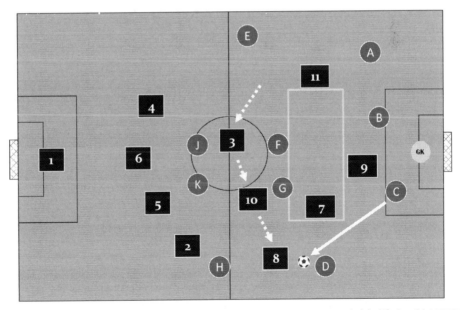

(8) leaves (G) to press (D). (10) leaves (F) to Press (G). (3) drops back in to mark (F). (8) should ANTICIPATE the pass to (D) and move quickly, other players behind him follow suit. Try to overload around the ball.

This is what could also happen

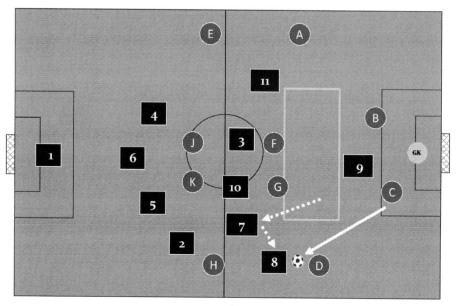

(8) may even delay (D) to allow (7) to recover back as well so we get the overload we want. Imagine players are tied together with a rope and they HAVE to move together in sync. Leave the far players (E) and (A) free.

8. We defend too deep from free kicks

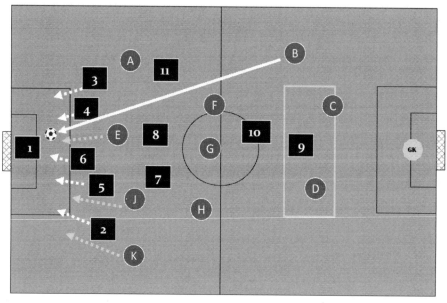

Defending on the edge of our box, our defenders are too close to the keeper so there is no room for him to come and claim the ball played in behind.

Keeper has very little space to come and catch

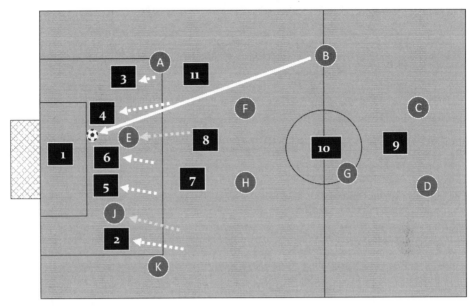

With a too deep start position this is where it could end up, a big advantage to the opponents.

What we should do

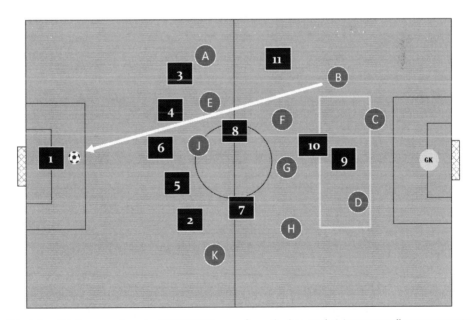

We defend higher now, keeping EVERYONE away from the box and giving our goalkeeper room to comfortably handle any ball played in behind our defense.

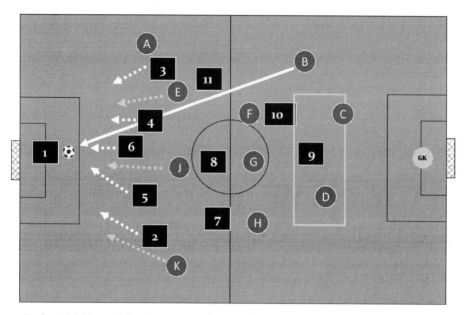

The result of establishing a higher line. Even with our defenders dropping 10 yards or so, there is plenty of room for our goalkeeper to claim the long delivery.

What could also happen from defending high

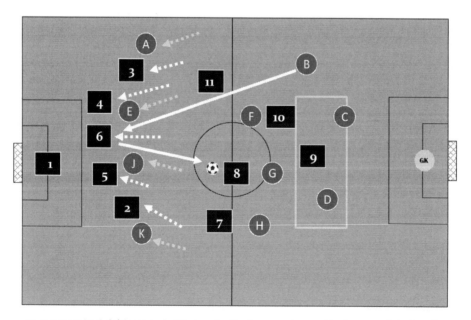

Now center back (6) has headed it clear for the team and saves the keeper a lot of work.

9. They get the ball out and keep possession; we have to press and also recover at the same time

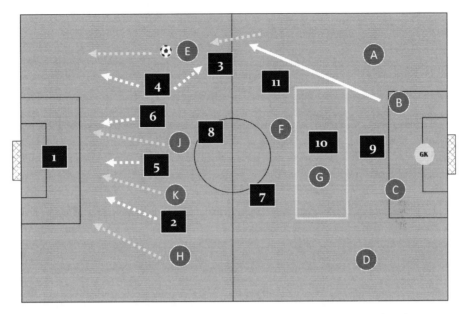

We've allowed ourselves to be beaten 1 v 1 which means we do not delay the attack and our recovering players cannot get back in time...JOCKEY; HOLD UP; FORCE WIDE.

Defender must delay and force him wide

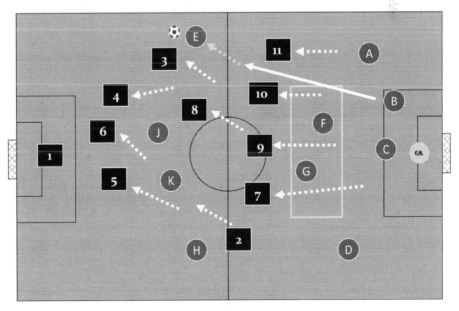

(3) forces (E) wide, stays on his feet and delays the attack. We recover in straight lines or the shortest route back to goal; or to the ball.

10. We don't press together as a unit in the Attacking Third

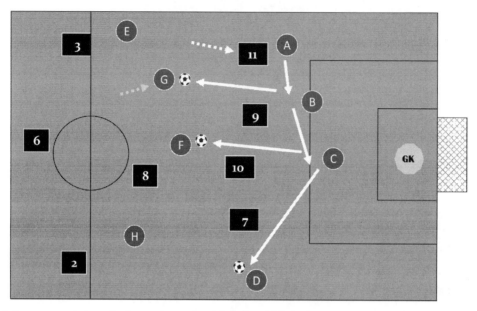

(11) presses and stops the forward pass; but (9), (10) and (7) don't. So the opponents get out easily.
One pass kills 4 of our players and now they are out of the game.

We press but only one at a time as a unit

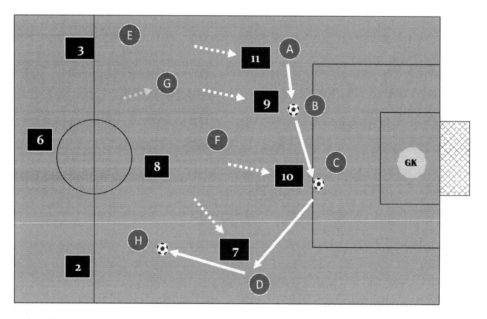

This is better, (11) presses; then (9), then (10) and then (7), but "one at a time", not together.
So the opponents still get out too easily.

The RIGHT WAY: We press together as a unit

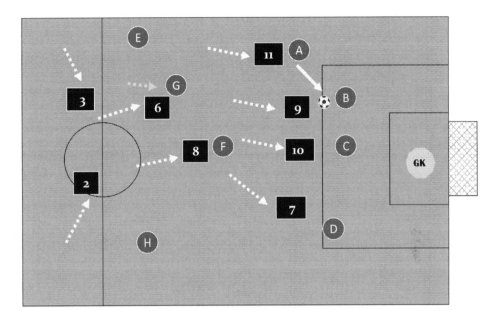

Four players press together up front and stop them getting out and may ultimately win the ball and get a goal scoring chance. The player on the ball (A) has no options. (11) forces him inside to where the pressure is.

11. We lose the ball with a bad pass and are vulnerable to the counter attack

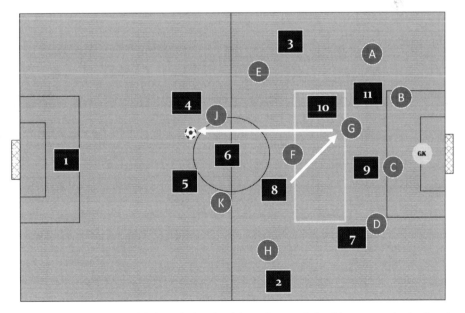

Both wing backs are attacking. (6) doesn't drop back in and we are left with a 2 v 2 at the back and so we allow ourselves to be vulnerable to the counter attack.

We stop it "very simply" like this

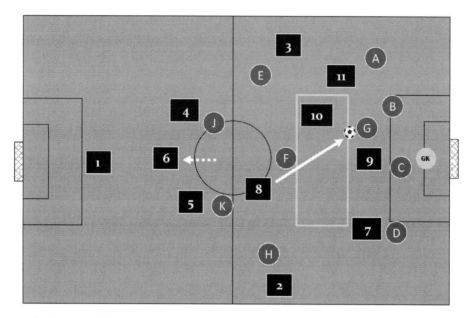

We are caught having to defend and we need to get our defensive discipline immediately fixed. Here (6) must drop in immediately to make a 3 v 2. Hence when both wing backs attack (6) MUST stay close to (4) and (5).

12. Wide players do not recover leaving a 2 v 1 against

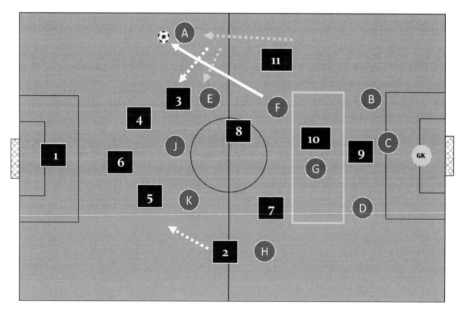

A common one. Here (11) does not recover back. (E) takes (3) inside to create a 2 v 1 against him.

This is what should happen

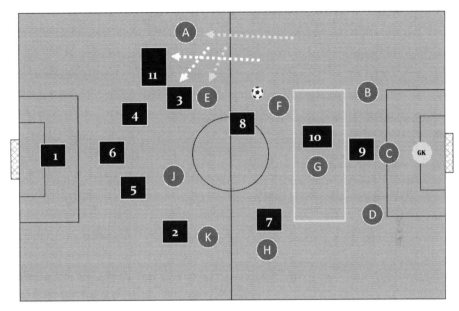

Here (11) tracks back and fills the space so (F) cannot make the pass. At academy level many teams use this ploy of attacking; we must defend effectively against it.

Or this

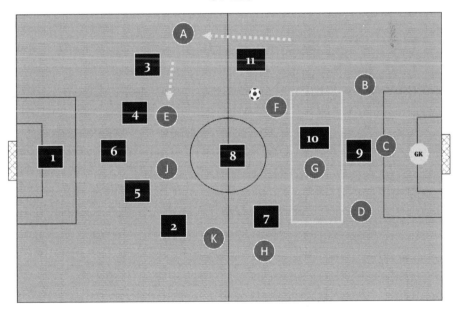

Good communication and (3) can pass on (E) to (4) and fill the space wide himself. But they MUST TALK !! Both ways can work as shown.

Conclusion

The 3-3-1-3 offers up great fluidity of movement for the players within the units and between the units. It can be a slightly more offensive set up than the 4-2-3-1. For the changes in set up per the game situation, it is all very subjective and there isn't one particular best way to do it. But I think if we have a basic plan for each situation as I have shown, we then have a starting point for discussion and each coach can determine how to use it in any particular game situation.

One final point: if opposition coaches were aware of what we do for these situations then they can work out what we change and counter, but as we know what we are doing in advance, we can potentially catch them out in the moment.